STATE-BUILDING

STATE-BUILDING

GOVERNANCE
AND WORLD ORDER
IN THE 21ST CENTURY

FRANCIS FUKUYAMA

CORNELL UNIVERSITY PRESS
ITHACA, NEW YORK

First published 2004 by Cornell University Press

Printed in the United States of America

Library of Congress Cataloging-in-Publication Data
Fukuyama, Francis.
   State-building : governance and world order in the 21st century / Francis Fukuyama.
     p. cm.
   Includes bibliographical references and index.
   ISBN 0-8014-4292-3 (cloth : alk. paper)
   1. State, The. 2. National state. I. Title.
JA66.F85 2004
320.1—dc22

                                        2004000905

Cornell University Press strives to use environmentally responsible suppliers and materials to the fullest extent possible in the publishing of its books. Such materials include vegetable-based, low-VOC inks and acid-free papers that are recycled, totally chlorine-free, or partly composed of nonwood fibers. For further information, visit our website at www.cornellpress.cornell.edu.

Cloth printing   10 9 8 7 6

To Marty Lipset

CONTENTS

PREFACE

State-building is the creation of new government institutions and the strengthening of existing ones. In this book I argue that state-building is one of the most important issues for the world community because weak or failed states are the source of many of the world's most serious problems, from poverty to AIDS to drugs to terrorism. I also argue that while we know a lot about state-building, there is a great deal we don't know, particularly about how to transfer strong institutions to developing countries. We know how to transfer resources across international borders, but well-functioning public institutions require certain habits of mind and operate in complex ways that resist being moved. We need to focus a great deal more thought, attention, and research on this area.

The idea that state-building, as opposed to limiting or cutting back the state, should be at the top of our agenda may strike some people as perverse. The dominant trend in world politics for the past generation has been, after all, the critique of "big government" and the attempt to move activities from the state sector to private markets or to civil society. But particularly in the developing world, weak, incompetent, or non-existent government is the source of severe problems.

For example, the AIDS epidemic in Africa has infected more than 25 million people and will take a staggering toll of lives. AIDS can be treated, as it has been in the developed world, with antiretroviral drugs. There has been a strong push to provide public funding for AIDS medicine or to force pharmaceutical companies to permit the marketing of cheaper forms of their products in Africa and other parts of the Third World. While part of the AIDS problem is a matter of resources, another important aspect is government capacity to administer health programs. Antiretroviral drugs are not only expensive, they also are complex to administer. Unlike a one-shot vaccine, they must be taken in complex doses over a long period of time; failure to follow the regimen may actually make the epidemic worse by allowing the human immunodeficiency virus to mutate and develop drug resistance. Effective treatment requires a strong public health infrastructure, public education, and knowledge about the epidemiology of the disease in specific regions. Even if the resources were there, the institutional capacity to treat the disease is lacking in many countries in sub-Saharan Africa (though some, like Uganda, have done a much better job than others). Dealing with this epidemic thus requires helping afflicted countries develop the institutional capacity to use what resources they may acquire.

Lack of state capacity in poor countries has come to haunt the developed world much more directly. The end of the Cold War left a band of failed and weak states stretching from the Balkans through the Caucasus, the Middle East, Central Asia, and South Asia. State collapse or weakness had already created major humanitarian and human rights disasters during the 1990s in Somalia, Haiti, Cambodia, Bosnia, Kosovo, and East Timor. For a while, the United States and other countries could pretend these problems were just local, but September

11 proved that state weakness constituted a huge strategic challenge as well. Radical Islamist terrorism combined with the availability of weapons of mass destruction added a major security dimension to the burden of problems created by weak governance. The United States has taken on major new responsibilities for nation-building in Afghanistan and Iraq in the wake of military actions there. Suddenly the ability to shore up or create from whole cloth missing state capabilities and institutions has risen to the top of the global agenda and seems likely to be a major condition for security in important parts of the world. Thus state weakness is both a national and an international issue of the first order.

This book has three main parts. The first lays out an analytical framework for understanding the multiple dimensions of "stateness"—that is, the functions, capabilities, and grounds for legitimacy of governments. This framework will explain why, in most developing countries, states are not too strong but rather too weak. The second part looks at the causes of state weakness, particularly why there can be no science of public administration despite recent efforts by economists to establish one. This lack sharply limits the ability of outsiders to help countries strengthen their state capacity. The final part discusses the international dimensions of state weakness: how instability is driven by state weakness, how weakness has eroded the principle of sovereignty in the international system, and how questions of democratic legitimacy on an international level have come to dominate disputes between the United States, Europe, and other developed countries in the international system.

This book is based on the Messenger Lectures I delivered at Cornell University in Ithaca, New York, February 18–21, 2003. I am very grateful to Cornell, my undergraduate alma mater, and its former president, Hunter Rawlings, for inviting me to return and deliver this prestigious series. I particularly appreciate the efforts of Victor Nee of the Sociology Department at Cornell to facilitate the lecture series and host me at the newly formed Center for the Study of Economy and Society and those of the Center's associate director, Richard Swedberg.

Parts of Chapter 3 were given as the John Bonython lecture in Melbourne, Australia, and the Sir Ronald Trotter Lecture delivered in Wellington, New Zealand, both in August 2002. I am grateful to the Centre for Independent Studies and its director, Greg Lindsey, and to Roger Kerr and Catherine Judd of the New Zealand Business Roundtable for helping bring my family and me to their part of the world. Owen Harries, former editor of *The National Interest*, also provided valuable comments on the lecture.

Many of the ideas in this book came from a graduate course on comparative politics that I taught with Seymour Martin Lipset over a period of several years at the School of Public Policy at George Mason University. I have learned an enormous amount from Marty Lipset over the years, and it is to him that this book is dedicated.

I received helpful comments and advice from a number of friends and colleagues, including Roger Leeds, Jessica Einhorn, Fred Starr, Enzo Grilli, Michael Mandelbaum, Robert Klitgaard, John Ikenberry, Michael Ignatieff, Peter Boettke, Rob Chase, Martin Shefter, Jeremy Rabkin, Brian Levy, Gary Hamel, Liisa Välikangas, Richard Pascale, Chet Crocker, Grace Goodell, Marc Plattner, and Karen Macours.

Parts of the lectures on which the book is based were also given at the Inter-American Development Bank and the U.S. Agency for International Development; I would like to thank Enrique Iglesias, president of the IDB, and Ann Phillips of USAID's Bureau for Policy and Program Coordination for facilitating these events. Presentations of parts of Chapter 3 were also made at the Miller Center at the University of Virginia, the Carr Center at Harvard's Kennedy School of Government, the Transatlantic Center at SAIS, the Maxwell School at Syracuse University, and the German Marshall Fund.

My research assistants Matthias Matthijs, Krisztina Csiki, Matt Miller, and particularly Björn Dressel provided great assistance in putting together materials for the book. My assistant, Cynthia Doroghazi, was helpful in many different phases of the project.

As always, I thank my family for their support through the writing of this book.

STATE-BUILDING

THE MISSING DIMENSIONS
OF STATENESS

The state is an ancient human institution dating back some 10,000 years to the first agricultural societies that sprang up in Mesopotamia. In China a state with a highly trained bureaucracy has existed for thousands of years. In Europe the modern state, deploying large armies, taxation powers, and a centralized bureaucracy that could exercise sovereign authority over a large territory, is much more recent, dating back four or five hundred years to the consolidation of the French, Spanish, and Swedish monarchies. The rise of these states, with their ability to provide order, security, law, and property rights, was what made possible the rise of the modern economic world.

States have a wide variety of functions, for good and ill. The same coercive power that allows them to protect property rights and provide public safety also allows them to confiscate private property and abuse the rights of their citizens. The monopoly of legitimate power that states exercise allows individuals to escape what Hobbes labeled the "war of every man against every man" domestically but serves as the basis for conflict and war at an international level. The task of modern politics has been to tame the power of the state, to direct its activities toward ends regarded as legitimate by the people it serves, and to regularize the exercise of power under a rule of law.

Modern states in this sense are anything but universal. They did not exist at all in large parts of the world like sub-Saharan Africa before European colonialism. After World War II decolonization led to a flurry of state-building all over the developing world, which was successful in countries like India and China but which occurred in name only in many other parts of Africa, Asia, and the Middle East. The last European empire to collapse—that of the former Soviet Union—initiated much the same process, with varying and often equally troubled results.

The problem of weak states and the need for state-building have thus existed for many years, but the September 11 attacks made them more obvious. Poverty is not the proximate cause of terrorism: The organizers of the attacks on the World Trade Center and the Pentagon on that date came from middle-class backgrounds and indeed were radicalized not in their native countries but in Western Europe. However, the attacks brought attention to a central problem for the West: The modern world offers a very attractive package, combining the material prosperity of market economies and the political and cultural freedom of liberal democracy. It is a package that very many people in the world want, as evidenced by the largely one-way flows of immigrants and refugees from less-developed to more-developed countries.

But the modernity of the liberal West is difficult to achieve for many societies around the world. While some countries in East Asia have made this transition successfully over the past two generations, others in the developing world have either been stuck or have actually regressed over this period. At issue is whether the institutions and values of the liberal West are indeed universal, or whether they represent, as Samuel Huntington (1996) would argue, merely the outgrowth of cultural habits of a certain part of the northern European world. The fact that Western governments and multilateral development agencies have not been able to provide much in terms of useful advice or help to developing countries undercuts the higher ends they seek to foster.

The Contested Role of the State

It is safe to say that politics in the twentieth century were heavily shaped by controversies over the appropriate size and strength of the state. The century began with a liberal world order presided over by the world's leading liberal state, Great Britain. The scope of state activity was not terribly broad in Britain or any of the other leading European powers, outside of the military realm, and in the United States, it was even narrower. There were no income taxes, poverty programs, or food safety regulations. As the century proceeded through war, revolution, depression, and war again, that liberal world order crumbled, and the minimalist liberal state was replaced throughout much of the world by a much more highly centralized and active one.

One stream of development lead to what Friedrich and Brzezinski (1965) labeled the "totalitarian" state, which tried to abolish the whole of civil society and subordinate the remaining atomized individuals to its own political ends. The right-wing version of this experiment ended in 1945 with the defeat of Nazi Germany, while the left-wing version crumbled under the weight of its own contradictions when the Berlin Wall fell in 1989.

The size, functions, and scope of the state increased in non-totalitarian countries as well, including virtually all democracies during the first three-quarters of the twentieth century. While state sectors at the beginning of the century consumed little more than 10 percent of gross domestic product (GDP) in most Western European countries and the United States, they consumed nearly 50 percent (70 percent in the case of social democratic Sweden) by the 1980s.

This growth, and the inefficiencies and unanticipated consequences it produced, led to a vigorous counterreaction in the form of "Thatcherism" and "Reaganism." The politics of the 1980s and 1990s were characterized by the reascendance of liberal ideas throughout much of the developed world, along with attempts to hold the line, if not reverse course, in terms of state-sector growth (Posner 1975). The collapse of the most extreme form of statism, communism, gave extra impetus to the movement to reduce the size of the state in noncommunist countries. Friedrich A. Hayek, who was pilloried at midcentury for suggesting that there was a connection between totalitarianism and the modern welfare state (Hayek 1956), saw his ideas taken much more seriously by the time of his death in 1992—not just in the political world, where conservative and center-right parties came to power, but in academia as well, where neoclassical economics gained enormously in prestige as the leading social science.

Reducing the size of the state sector was the dominant theme of policy during the critical years of the 1980s and early 1990s, when a wide variety of countries in the former communist world, Latin America, Asia, and Africa were emerging from authoritarian rule after what Huntington (1991) labeled the "third wave" of democratization. There was no question that the all-encompassing state sectors of the former communist world needed to be dramatically scaled back, but state bloat had infected many noncommunist developing countries as well. For example, the Mexican government's share of GDP expanded from 21 percent in 1970 to 48 percent in 1982, and its fiscal deficit reached 17 percent of GDP, laying the groundwork for the debt crisis that emerged that year (Krueger 1993, 11). The state sectors of many sub-Saharan African countries engaged in activities like running large state-owned corporations and agricultural marketing boards that had negative effects on productivity (Bates 1981, 1983).

In response to these trends, the advice offered by international financial institutions (IFIs) like the International Monetary Fund (IMF) and World Bank, as well as by the U.S. government, emphasized a collection of measures intended to reduce the degree of state intervention in economic affairs—a package designated as the "Washington consensus" by one of its formulators (Williamson 1994) or as "neoliberalism" by its detractors in Latin America. The Washington consensus has been relentlessly attacked in the early twenty-first century, not just by antiglobalization protesters but also by academic critics with better credentials in economics (see Rodrik 1997; Stiglitz 2002).

In retrospect, there was nothing wrong with the Washington consensus per se: The state sectors of developing countries were in very many cases obstacles to growth and could only be fixed in the long run through economic liberalization. Rather, the problem was that although states needed to be cut back in certain areas, they needed to be simultaneously strengthened in others. The economists who promoted liberalizing economic reform understood this perfectly well in theory. But the relative emphasis in this period lay very heavily on the reduction of state activity, which could often be confused or deliberately misconstrued as an effort to cut back state capacity across the board. The state-building agenda, which was at least as important as the state-reducing one, was not given nearly as much thought or emphasis. The result was that liberalizing economic reform failed to deliver on its promise in many countries. In some countries, indeed, absence of a proper institutional framework left them worse off after liberalization than they would have been in its absence. The problem lay in a basic conceptual failure to unpack the different dimensions of stateness and to understand how they related to economic development.

Scope versus Strength

I begin the analysis of the role of the state in development by posing this question: Does the United States have a strong or weak state? One clear-cut answer is that given by Lipset (1995): American institutions are deliberately designed to weaken or limit the exercise of state power. The United States was born in a revolution against state authority, and the resulting antistatist political culture was expressed in constraints on state power like constitutional government with clear-cut protections for individual rights, the separation of powers, federalism, and so forth. Lipset points out that the American welfare state was established later and remains much more limited (e.g., no comprehensive health care system) than those of other developed democracies, that markets are much less regulated, and that the United States was in the forefront of rolling back its welfare state in the 1980s and 1990s.

On the other hand, there is another sense in which the American state is very strong. Max Weber (1946) defined the state as "a human community that (successfully) claims the *monopoly of the legitimate use of physical force* within a given territory." The essence of stateness is, in other words, *enforcement*: the ultimate ability to send someone with a uniform and a gun to force people to comply with the state's laws. In this respect, the American state is extraordinarily strong: It has a plethora of enforcement agencies at federal, state, and local levels to enforce everything from traffic rules to commercial law to fundamental breaches of the Bill of Rights. Americans, for various complex reasons, are not a law-abiding people when compared to citizens of other developed democracies (Lipset 1990), but not for want of an extensive and often highly punitive criminal and civil justice system that deploys substantial enforcement powers.

The United States, in other words, has a system of limited government that has historically restricted the *scope* of state activity. Within that scope, its ability to create and enforce laws and policies is very strong. There is, of course, a great deal of justified cynicism on the part of many Americans about the efficiency and sensibility of their own government (see, for example, Howard 1996). But the American rule of law is the envy of much of the rest of the world: Those Americans who complain about how their local department of motor vehicles treats motorists should try getting a driver's license or dealing with a traffic violation in Mexico City or Jakarta.

It therefore makes sense to distinguish between the scope of state activities, which refers to the different functions and goals taken on by governments, and the strength of state power, or the ability of states to plan and execute policies and to enforce laws cleanly and transparently—what is now commonly referred to as state or institutional capacity. One of the confusions in our understanding of stateness is that the word *strength* is often used indifferently to refer both to what is here labeled *scope* as well as to *strength* or *capacity*.

Distinguishing between these two dimensions of stateness allows us to create a matrix that helps differentiate the degrees of stateness in a variety of countries around the world. We can array the scope of state activities along a continuum that stretches from necessary and important to merely desirable to optional, and in certain cases counterproductive or even destructive. There is of course no agreed-on hierarchy of state functions, particularly when it comes to issues like redistribution and social policy. Most people would agree that there has to be *some* degree of hierarchy: States need to provide public order and defense from external invasion before they provide universal health insurance or free higher education. The World Bank's 1997 *World Development Report* (World Bank 1997) provides one plausible list of state functions, divided into three categories that range from "minimal" to "intermediate" to "activist" (Figure 1). This list is obviously not exhaustive but provides useful benchmarks for state scope.

If we take these functions and array them along an X-axis as in Figure 2, we can then locate different countries at different points along the axis depending on how ambitious they are in terms of what their governments seek to accomplish. There are of course countries that attempt complex governance tasks like running parastatals or allocating investment credits, while being unable to provide basic public goods like law and order or public infrastructure. We will array countries along this axis according to the most ambitious types of functions they seek to perform.

There is a completely separate Y-axis, which represents the strength of institutional capabilities. Strength in this sense includes, as noted above, the ability to formulate and carry out policies and enact laws; to administrate efficiently and with a mini-

	Addressing market failure				Improving equity
Minimal functions	Providing pure public goods				Protecting the poor
	Defense				Antipoverty programs
	Law and order				Disaster relief
	Property rights				
	Macroeconomic management				
	Public health				
Intermediate functions	Addressing externalities:	Regulating monopoly:	Overcoming imperfect information:		Providing social insurance:
	education	utility regulation	insurance		redistributive pensions
	environmental protection	anti-trust	financial regulation		family allowances
			consumer protection		unemployment insurance
Activist functions	Coordinating private activity:				Redistribution:
	fostering markets				asset redistribution
	cluster initiatives				

Figure 1. Functions of the state. (Source: World Bank, World Development Report, 1997).

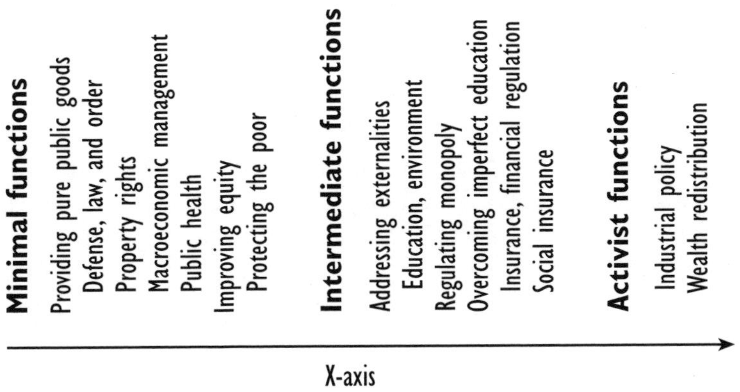

Minimal functions							**Intermediate functions**							**Activist functions**		
Providing pure public goods	Defense, law, and order	Property rights	Macroeconomic management	Public health	Improving equity	Protecting the poor		Addressing externalities	Education, environment	Regulating monopoly	Overcoming imperfect education	Insurance, financial regulation	Social insurance		Industrial policy	Wealth redistribution

X-axis

Figure 2. The scope of state functions.

mum of bureaucracy; to control graft, corruption, and bribery; to maintain a high level of transparency and accountability in government institutions; and, most important, to *enforce* laws.

There is obviously no commonly accepted measure for strength of state institutions. Different state agencies may be located at different points along this axis. A country like Egypt, for example, has a very effective internal security apparatus and yet cannot execute simple tasks like processing visa applications or licensing small businesses efficiently (Singerman 1995). Other countries like Mexico and Argentina have been relatively successful in reforming certain state institu-

tions like central banking but less so at controlling fiscal policy or providing high-quality public health or education. As a
result, state capacity may vary strongly across state functions
(Figure 3).

With the renewed emphasis on institutional quality in the
1990s, a number of relevant indices have been developed that
help locate countries along the Y-axis. One of these is the Corruption Perception Index developed by Transparency International, which is based on survey data primarily from the business communities operating in different countries. Another is
the privately produced International Country Risk Guide
Numbers, which are broken down into separate measures of
corruption, law and order, and bureaucratic quality. In addition, the World Bank has developed governance indicators cov-
ering 199 countries (Kaufmann, Kraay, and Mastruzzi 2003;
indicators for six aspects of governance are available at www
.worldbank.org/wbi/governance/govdata2002). There are also
broader measures of political rights like Freedom House's index

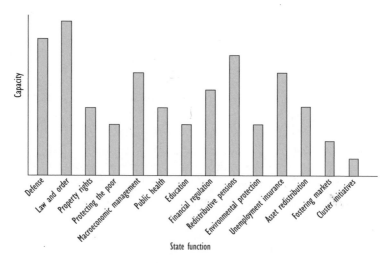

Figure 3. State capacity (hypothetical).

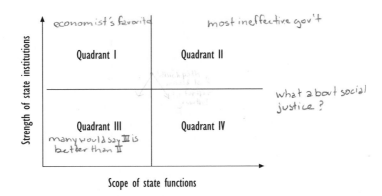

Figure 4. Stateness and efficiency.

of political freedom and civil liberties, which aggregates democracy and individual rights into a single guide number, and the Polity IV data on regime characteristics.[1]

If we combine these two dimensions of scope and strength into a single graph, we get a matrix like that in Figure 4. The matrix divides neatly into four quadrants that have very different consequences for economic growth. From the economists's standpoint, the optimal place to be is in quadrant I, which combines limited scope of state functions with strong institutional effectiveness. Economic growth will cease, of course, if a state moves too far toward the origin of the axis and fails to perform minimal functions like protecting property rights, but the presumption is that growth will fall as states move farther to the right along the X-axis.

Economic success is not, of course, the only reason for preferring a given scope of state functions; many Europeans argue that American-style efficiency comes at the price of social justice and that they are happy to be in quadrant II rather than quadrant I. On the other hand, the worst place to be in eco-

[1] This dataset is compiled by Monty Marshall and Keith Juggers and is available at www.cidcm.umd.edu/inscr/polity/.

nomic performance terms is in quadrant IV, where an ineffective state takes on an ambitious range of activities that it cannot perform well. Unfortunately, this is exactly where a large
number of developing countries are found.

I have located a number of countries within this matrix for
purposes of illustration (Figure 5). The United States, for example, has a less extensive state than either France or Japan; it
has not attempted the management of broad sectoral transitions through credit allocation as Japan did in its industrial
policy during the 1960s and 1970s, nor does it boast the same
kind of high-quality top-level bureaucracy like France with its
grands écoles. On the other hand, the quality of the U.S. bureaucracy is considerably higher than that of most developing
countries. Turkey and Brazil, by contrast, have funneled large
proportions of GDP through their state sectors, run national-
ized industries, and regulated and protected a wide range of
economic activities.

It is not possible to locate countries in the various quadrants
precisely, if for no other reason than that state capacity varies
within a single country across administrative agencies. Japan
has a less extensive welfare state than either France or Germany if we measure its size by outright income transfers or social programs. Instead, it uses regulation (e.g., protection of
small family-owned retail businesses) and certain microeconomic institutions like the seniority wage system and lifetime
employment in the private sector to provide an equivalent social safety net. However, Japan's industrial policies have been
historically more interventionist than those of most Western
European states, and its level of domestic regulation has been
very high. Thus, it is not clear whether it should be located to
the left or right of a typical European welfare state.

It should also be clear that countries can move within this
matrix over time. Indeed, one of the values of the matrix is
that it demonstrates the dynamic nature of changes in stateness. Thus the former Soviet Union went from being a state

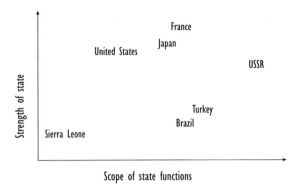

Figure 5. The stateness matrix.

with very extensive scope (e.g., no private property) and a moderate degree of strength in administrative capabilities to a state with a much narrower scope of functions and an equally diminished degree of state capacity. The same can be said for Japan over the past two decades: It has made hesitant efforts at market liberalization, privatizing some state-owned companies and deregulating some domestic industries (largely under international pressure) while seeing the quality of its much vaunted bureaucracies (in particularly, the finance ministry) deteriorate or be captured by societal interests. Hence, both Japan and the Soviet Union/Russian saw their state sectors move in the same southwesterly direction between approximately 1980 and 2000, though they obviously started from very different places and moved at very different speeds (Figure 6).

These cases stand in sharp contrast to that of New Zealand, which began a series of liberalizing reforms in the mid-1980s under the guidance of the Labour Party and its finance minister, Roger Douglas. By the early 1980s New Zealand had developed one of the world's most extensive welfare states, but it was clearly heading for crisis with the ballooning of national

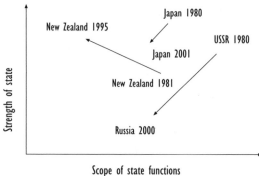

Figure 6. Change over time in strength of state institutions and scope of state functions.

debt and a steady decline in the current account. The initial set of reforms begun in 1984 floated the New Zealand dollar; abolished currency controls, agricultural and consumer subsidies, import licenses, and export incentives; changed the tax structure from income and sales taxes to a broad-based consumption tax; and privatized state industries (New Zealand State Services Commission 1998). All were classic measures to reduce the scope of the state in New Zealand. But with passage of the State Sector Act in 1988, a second phase of the reform began that sought to strengthen the administrative capacity of those core state agencies that remained. These reforms required departments to file monthly financial reports using commercial accounting standards, put them under the direction of chief executives who were hired under term contracts that set out conditions for employment, increased managerial discretion to permit shifting of the mix of inputs to be used to produce agreed outputs, and established a system of accountability using contract-like arrangements within the government (Schick 1996; Boston et al. 1996). Thus, New Zealand had, by the mid-1990s, moved in preferred northwesterly direction.

Scope, Strength, and Economic Development

The development agenda for many IFIs shifted dramatically in the 1990s in a way that can be illustrated as follows. There is no question that it is better to be in quadrant I than in quadrant IV, but is it better to be in quadrant II, with strong institutions and an extensive state, or quadrant III, with weak institutions and a limited state? In the early 1990s many economists preferred quadrant III on the grounds that markets would be self-organizing or that institutions and residual state capabilities would somehow take care of themselves. The so-called Washington consensus was a perfectly sensible list of economic policy measures that were designed to move countries leftward along the X-axis through reduced tariff protection, privatization, reduction of subsidies, deregulation, and so forth. There is no reason, after all, for the Brazilian government to operate steel mills or for Argentina to create a domestic automobile industry. In many cases, transitional and emerging-market countries were advised to move as rapidly as possible toward smaller state scope on the grounds that the political window for engaging in this kind of reform would close quickly and that it was better to get the pain of adjustment over with all at once.

The problem for many countries was that in the process of reducing state scope they either decreased state strength or generated demands for new types of state capabilities that were either weak or nonexistent. The austerity required by stabilization and structural adjustment policies became, in certain countries, an excuse for cutting state capacity across the board, and not just in activities on the right side of the X-axis. In other words, while the optimal reform path would have been to decrease scope while increasing strength (path I in Figure 7), many countries actually decreased both scope and strength, moving in a southeasterly direction (path II). Instead of ending up in quadrant I, they ended up in quadrant III.

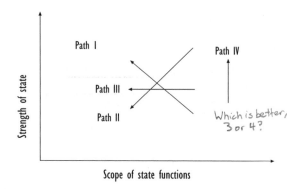

Figure 7. Reform paths

Change like this occurred in sub-Saharan Africa in the last quarter of the twentieth century. It is common to characterize regimes in sub-Saharan Africa as "neopatrimonial"— that is, with political power used to service a clientelistic network of supporters of the country's leaders (Joseph 1987; Fatton 1992). In some cases, as with Mobutu Sese Seko of Zaire, neopatrimonial regimes result in what Evans (1989) characterizes as "predatory" behavior, where a large part of society's resources are stolen by a single individual. In others, it merely amounts to rent-seeking—that is, use of the public sector to reallocate property rights to the benefit of a particular interest—that is directed toward a single family, tribe, region, or ethnic group. As van de Walle (2001) points out, the neopatrimonial regime, usually embodied in the office of the president, exists side-by-side with a Weberian rational bureaucracy, often created in colonial times, that seeks to perform routine public administration tasks. The neopatrimonial network is often threatened by the existence of the modern state sector and is its competitor for resources.

The dual nature of such an African state meant that donor-imposed stabilization and structural adjustment programs during the 1980s and 1990s had an unintended and counterproductive effect. The international lending community called for cutbacks in state scope through implementation of orthodox adjustment and liberalization programs, but given their ultimate political dominance, neopatrimonial regimes used external conditionality as an excuse for cutting back on the modern state sectors while protecting and often expanding the scope of the neopatrimonial state. Thus, investment in basic infrastructure like roads and public health declined dramatically over a twenty-year period, as well as investments in primary education and agriculture. At the same time, spending on so-called sovereignty expenditures like military forces, diplomatic services, and jobs connected to the office of the presidency increased dramatically. (In Kenya, for example, the employees of the office of the president grew from 18,213 in 1971 to 43,230 in 1990.) No international lender or bilateral donor at any time wanted this outcome, yet none were able to structure their conditionality in a way to prevent it from happening because of their inability to control local political outcomes.

Many proponents of the Washington consensus now say that they *of course* understood the importance of institutions, rule of law, and the proper sequencing of reforms. But Y-axis questions of state capacity and state-building were largely absent from policy discussion in the late 1980s to early 1990s. There were very few warnings issued from Washington-based policymakers about the dangers of liberalization in the absence of proper institutions. Indeed, the general inclination among policymakers at the time was that any degree of liberalization was likely to be better than no liberalization at all.[2]

---

[2] This characterized the thinking of Clinton administration officials at the time of the South Korean entry into the Organisation for Economic Co-operation and Development (OECD) and in policy toward Thailand in the early 1990s, for example, when there was little evidence of warnings concerning premature capital account liberalization. See David Sanger and Nicholas Kristof, "How U.S. Wooed Asia To Let Cash Flow In," *New York Times*, 16 Feb. 1999, sec. A, p. 1.

It took the Asian economic crisis of 1997–98 and the problems experienced by Russia and other postcommunist countries for thinking on these issues to begin to shift. The financial crises experienced by Thailand and South Korea were both directly linked to premature capital account liberalization in the absence of adequate regulatory institutions that could oversee domestic banking sectors that were suddenly flooded with enormous amounts of foreign short-term capital (Lanyi and Lee 1999; Haggard 2000). It is clear in retrospect that under these circumstances, a little liberalization can be more dangerous than no liberalization at all. South Korea, for example, liberalized its capital account as a condition for entry into the OECD without a corresponding opening of its equity markets or greater foreign direct investment. As a result, foreign investors who wanted to get a piece of the Korean economic miracle had their money in short-term accounts that could be withdrawn at the first sign of trouble. When South Korea's current account began to deteriorate in 1996–97, the currency came under irresistible pressure as short-term capital was withdrawn. This situation set the stage for the economic crisis of late 1997.

The problem in Russia and other postcommunist countries was somewhat different. The privatization of state-owned enterprises is of course an appropriate goal of economic reform, but it requires a substantial degree of institutional capacity to implement properly. Privatization inevitably creates huge information asymmetries, and it is the job of governments to correct them. Assets and ownership rights have to be properly identified, valued, and transferred transparently; the rights of new minority shareholders have to be protected to prevent asset-stripping, tunneling, and other abuses. Thus, while privatization involves a reduction in the scope of state functions, it requires functioning markets and a high degree of state capacity to implement. This capacity did not exist in Russia, with the result that many privatized assets did not end up in the hands of entrepreneurs who could make them productive. The stealing of public resources by the so-called oligarchs did much to delegitimate the post-communist Russian state. This new recognition of the priority of strength over scope is reflected in a comment made by Milton Friedman, dean of orthodox free market economists, in 2001. He noted that a decade earlier he would have had three words for countries making the transition from socialism: "privatize, privatize, privatize." "But I was wrong," he continued. "It turns out that the rule of law is probably more basic than privatization" (interview with Milton Friedman, Gwartney and Lawson 2002).

From the standpoint of economic efficiency, is it more important to reduce state scope or increase state strength? In other words, if a country was forced to choose between paths III and IV in Figure 7, which would lead to greater growth? It is, of course, impossible to generalize, since economic performance will depend on the specific institutional capacities and state functions in question, as well as on a host of other factors. There is evidence, however, that strength of state institutions is more important in a broad sense than the scope of state functions. We have, after all, the growth record of Western Europe, whose scope of state functions is far larger than that of the United States but whose institutions are strong as well. I have argued elsewhere (Fukuyama and Marwah 2000) that the reason for the superior performance of East Asia compared to Latin America over the past forty years is likely due more to the superior quality of state institutions in the former region than to any differences in state scope. The high-performing economies of East Asia vary tremendously with regard to state scope, ranging from minimalist Hong Kong to highly interventionist South Korea, whose average level of domestic protection during its high-growth period was as high as Argentina's (Amsden 1989). All of these countries nonetheless achieved extraordinarily high rates of per capita GDP growth. By contrast,

Latin America as a region scores worse than Asia on virtually every dimension of governance.

A further reason for thinking that state strength is more important than scope in determining long-term economic growth rates is that there is a fairly strong positive correlation across a wide variety of countries between per capita GDP and the percentage of GDP extracted by governments (Figure 8). That is, richer countries tend to be ones that funnel higher proportions of national wealth through their state sectors (World Bank 2002). The rate of tax extraction is, of course, a measure of state scope, particularly for countries with higher levels of per capita GDP, but it is also a measure of administrative capacity (and is increasingly used as a metric by IFIs). That is, there are any number of countries that would like to be able to take in a higher proportion of GDP in taxes but are unable to do so because they cannot monitor tax compliance and enforce tax laws. That a strong positive correlation exists between tax extraction and level of development suggests that overall, the

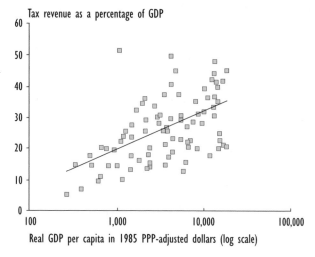

Figure 8. Tax extraction rates versus per capita gross domestic product.

negative effects of excessive state scope are in the long-run counterbalanced by the positive effects of greater administrative capacity.[3]

The New Conventional Wisdom

Much of what has been laid out about the importance of state strength is now taken for granted within the development policy community, whose mantra since at least 1997 has been the dictum that "institutions matter" (World Bank 1997, World Bank 2001). The concern over state strength, which goes under a variety of headings including "governance," "state capacity," or "institutional quality," has always been around under different titles in development economics. It was highlighted in Hernando de Soto's book *The Other Path* (1989), which reminded the development community of the importance of formal property rights and, more broadly, of the consequences of well-functioning legal institutions for efficiency. De Soto (1989, 134) sent his researchers to find out how long it took to get a small business license in Lima, Peru; 10 months, 11 offices, and $1231 later, they came back with legal authorization to start a business. The same process in the United States or Canada would take less than two days. The inefficiency of this process was a significant barrier to new business formation, and de Soto observed that it forced poor entrepreneurs into an informal sector. That informal sector was dynamic and often served as the only source for certain goods and services in poor neighborhoods, but the lack of formal, enforceable property rights reduced investment horizons and prevented small businesses from becoming big ones.

The development policy community thus finds itself in an

---

[3] Some forms of taxation are unambiguously bad for growth, such as tariffs and other taxes on international trade (World Bank 2002).

ironic position. The post–Cold War era began under the intellectual dominance of economists, who pushed strongly for liberalization and a smaller state. Ten years later, many economists have concluded that some of the most important variables affecting development weren't economic at all but were concerned with institutions and politics. There was an entire missing dimension of stateness that needed to be explored—that of state-building—an aspect of development that had been ignored in the single-minded focus on state scope. Many economists found themselves dusting off fifty-year-old books on public administration, or else reinventing the wheel to develop anticorruption strategies.

It is now conventional wisdom to say that institutions are the critical variable in development, and over the past few years a whole host of studies have provided empirical documentation that this is so (see, among others, Robinson and Acemoglu 2000; Easterly 2001; van de Walle 2001). There has, in addition, been a large and evolving literature on institutions and institutional development (see Klitgaard 1995; Grindle 1997, 2000; Tendler 1997; World Bank 1997, 2000, 2002).

All forms of "conventional wisdom" should make us cautious. Woolcock and Pritchett (2002) talk about the problem of "getting to Denmark," where "Denmark" stands generically for a developed country with well-functioning state institutions. We know what "Denmark" looks like, and something about how the actual Denmark came to be historically. But to what extent is that knowledge transferable to countries as far away historically and culturally from Denmark as Somalia or Moldova? To what extent is there and can there be a theory of institutions that can be generalized and that will provide the basis for policy guidance to poor countries?

Let us back up to the prior problem of unpacking what is currently meant by the term *institutions*. With the unfolding of development studies's linear space into multiple higher dimensions since the early 1990s, the field has become in many ways chaotic. Democracy, federalism, decentralization, participation, social capital, culture, gender, ethnicity, and ethnic conflict have all been added to the development pot as ingredients bearing on the final taste of the stew (Einhorn 2001). Are all of these concepts aspects of institutional development, and if so, in what ways? Are they of equal priority? Are they related to one another? And in what ways do they promote development?

The Supply of Institutions

If the central issue we are trying to understand is institutional capacity, we can begin on the supply side, with the question of what institutions are critical for economic development and how they ought to be designed. There are four nested aspects of stateness that we need to address: (1) organizational design and management, (2) political system design, (3) basis of legitimization, and (4) cultural and structural factors.

Organizational Design and Management

Need talented, educated, accredited individuals in every sector of the bureaucracy

The first level of organizational design and management corresponds to the domain of management studies (and business schools) when applied to the private sector, and of public administration vis à vis the public sector. Public administration is a large and well-developed field that consists of a host of specialized subdisciplines. It is a body of expertise in which one can readily receive training and accreditation. Although there have been repeated efforts to formalize knowledge about organizations into a body of theory akin to microeconomic theory (indeed, some economists see it as a branch of microeconomics), these efforts have not be totally satisfying. In Chapter 2 of this book, I discuss the question of the state of public administration studies and why there cannot be a unified theory of organizations.

Political System Design

The second aspect of stateness has to do with institutional design at the level of the state as a whole rather than the individual agencies that compose it. Again, this is a huge area of knowledge that in many respects corresponds to the field of political science broadly speaking. Political science focused on the design of political and legal institutions during the pre–World War II period, an approach that was eclipsed during the next generation by more sociological and structural interpretations of institutions and their functionality. Before the 1980s it was common to assert that institutions didn't matter or were themselves determined by the economic and social "substructure." Institutionalism has made something of a comeback in recent years, however, within the subfield of comparative politics, with numerous studies of the consequences for economic growth of parliamentary versus presidential systems, various types of electoral systems, federalism, party systems, and so forth (see, for example, Cowhey and Haggard 2001).

To an even greater extent than public administration or organizational theory, the existing body of knowledge concerning institutional design at the state level yields little by way of formal theory or universally applicable principles of political economy. Such theory as there is tends to talk about tradeoffs between various political design goals such as "representativeness" and "governability" (see, for example, Diamond 1990), between unity of purpose and checks and balances (Haggard and McCubbins 2001), or between dispersed and concentrated power (MacIntyre 2003). Since economic goals compete with other ones like fair distribution or ethnic balance in most societies, there can be no optimal set of institutions, but only institutions that tend to favor one set of goods over another. Moreover, the same institution can promote or detract from economic growth depending on whether there are complementary institutions that promote its functionality. For example, federalism and decentralization have been widely touted as ways of making government more responsive politically and more supportive of economic growth (see, for example, Weingast 1993). But in Russia, poor tax enforcement led to the competition of local governments with the federal government for revenues from the same tax base (World Bank 2002). Since the local level had better access to information, the result was a collapse of tax revenues during the 1990s at the federal level. Fiscal federalism is one of the reasons that Argentina has had such difficulty controlling budget deficits (Saiegh and Tommas 1998), a problem that has also plagued Brazil.

Similarly complex results may result depending on the design of executive branch institutions. Juan Linz (1990) inaugurated a prolonged debate over the relative merits of presidential versus parliamentary systems, arguing that presidentialism with its winner-take-all voting and fixed terms tended to promote instability and illegitimacy in Latin America and other regions where it was a prominent feature of constitutional design. Other observers pointed out that it was not presidentialism per se but rather the type of electoral system used in the legislative branch that frequently led to major problems like political gridlock (e.g., the combination of a presidential system with legislative proportional representation that is typical in much of Latin America—see Horowitz 1990; Lijphart 1996; Lardeyret 1996; Cowhey and Haggard 2001). Tendencies toward rent-seeking and pork-barrel politics are encouraged under a number of conditions, such as multimember electoral districts, geographically small constituencies, and open-list proportional representation, though the embedding of patronage in the party system depends heavily on the historical sequencing of franchise expansion and bureaucratic reform (Shefter 1993). All of this research leads to a realistic contextual richness but a relatively limited clear-cut theory of optimal political system design.

Basis of Legitimization

The third aspect of stateness is closely related to the question of systemic institutional design but goes beyond it by including a normative dimension—that is, the state's institutions not only have to work together properly as a whole in an administrative sense, they also have to be perceived as being legitimate by the underlying society. Samuel Huntington's *Political Order in Changing Societies* (1968) argued that the two could be separated: Countries could govern and acquire attributes of stateness independent of their basis of legitimation. Thus, for him, the former Soviet Union and the United States both were highly politically developed societies, despite the fact that one was a communist dictatorship and the other a liberal democracy. A more recent version of this argument has been made by Zakaria (2003), though the author emphasizes liberal rule-of-law rather than authoritarian administrative capacity.

With the hindsight of more than thirty years, it is not clear whether state capacity (or political development, in Huntington's terminology) can be separated from legitimacy all that easily. At the end of the 1980s the Soviet Union began collapsing and losing substantial amounts of state capacity precisely because its dictatorial character delegitimated the regime in the eyes of its citizens. Its apparent degree of political development was a Potemkin village, in other words, at the time that Huntington wrote *Political Order*. While there have historically been many forms of legitimacy, in today's world the only serious source of legitimacy is democracy.

There is another respect in which good governance and democracy are not so easily separated. A good state institution is one that transparently and efficiently serves the needs of its clients—the citizens of the state. In areas like monetary policy, the goals of policy are relatively straightforward (that is price stability) and can be met by relatively detached tech-

nocrats. Hence central banks are constructed in ways that deliberately shield them from short-term democratic political
pressure. In other sectors like primary and secondary education, the quality of the public agency's output greatly depends
on the feedback it receives from the ultimate consumers of
government services. It is hard to imagine technocrats working
in isolation from the people they serve doing a good job in
these areas. Hence democracy, apart from its legitimating
value, has a functional role in governance as well.

[margin handwriting: Thus, democracy is the necessary form of gov't]

There is an extensive literature that shows how development is related to democracy (see, among others, Lipset 1959;
Diamond 1992; Rowen 1995; Barro 1997; Roll and Talbott
2003). Przeworski and Alvarez (1996) argue that the level of development affects not the likelihood of transition to democracy but the likelihood of transition back into authoritarianism. But the reverse relationship—whether democracy helps or
hurts development—is what concerns us here, since we cannot
take successful development for granted. While the consensus
of opinion on this question has changed substantially over the
past generation, the relationship remains complex and not always positive.

There was a period in which various authors argued in favor
of an authoritarian transition (Huntington 1967), a view which
still finds some favor in East Asia, where it has worked relatively well. Many political economists assume that economic
reform requires austerity, job cuts, and other types of short-
term dislocations and therefore generates political opposition
and backlash. Reform is thus better undertaken by authoritarian regimes that can suppress societal demands, or else by a
technocratic elite that is somehow isolated or buffered from
political pressures. Haggard and Kaufmann (1995) see democratic transition as problematic because it releases pent-up demands for government benefits that contradict the goals of reform.

It has become much more fashionable in recent years to

argue with Sen (1999) that democracy is both an object of development in itself and a means toward economic growth. There are a number of reasons for this argument. It is clear, for example, that it is not authoritarianism per se that determines economic outcomes but rather the quality of the authoritarian leader and the technocrats advising him or her. Authoritarian countries as a group might do well if they could all be run by Lee Kwan Yew; given that they are as often run by a Mobutu or a Marcos, it is not surprising that authoritarian regimes show much greater variance than democratic ones in terms of development outcomes. Democratic regimes at least have some institutional checks against the worst forms of incompetence or rapacity: Bad leaders can be voted out of office.

Authoritarian countries, moreover, have long-term problems with legitimacy. Many have sought to legitimize themselves through their ability to deliver on growth, but when growth ceases or turns into decline (as was the case for Suharto's Indonesia in 1997–98), legitimacy disappears and instability ensues. Democratic countries are often better able to survive economic setbacks because their legitimacy comes from democracy itself (e.g., South Korea in 1997–98). At the same time, there have been significant examples of democratic countries like Poland or New Zealand making hard economic reform choices.

In the end, the empirical relationship between democracy and development remains complex and ambiguous: It does not support either authoritarian transitions as a general approach to economic reform or democratization as a growth strategy. Barro's (1997) cross-country survey shows that democracy is positively correlated with growth at low levels of development but then becomes negatively correlated at medium levels of per capita GDP. Patronage and rent-seeking (Turkey, Argentina, Brazil), populism (Venezuela), and corruption (Pakistan under Bhutto and Sharif) all remain democratic vices. It is hard to see a clear causal relationship between the wave of democratization that hit sub-Saharan Africa during the 1990s and the continent's slightly improved economic performance in this period.

Cultural and Structural Factors

The fourth aspect of stateness that is relevant to institutional capacity is subpolitical and related to norms, values, and culture. Much of the recent discussion of these issues within the development community has fallen under the rubric of social capital. Norms, values, and culture affect primarily the supply side of institutions by making possible or constraining certain types of formal institutions, though they affect the demand side as well by generating certain institutional needs or phobias.

It is usual to think of formal institutions, on the one hand, and informal norms or cultural values, on the other, as being quite separate conceptually and methodologically. (The institutional economics literature confusingly applies the word *institutions* to both formal and informal rules constraining individual choice; see North 1990). Chalmers Johnson (1982) argues that Japan's superior growth performance in its high-growth period was due not to culture (i.e., informal norms) but to formal institutions like industrial policies that in theory could be adopted by anyone. Formal rules can be readily changed as a matter of public policy; cultural rules cannot, and while they change over time, it is much harder to direct their development.

That Japan's relative success in running an industrial policy can be attributed to the existence of a certain set of formal institutions is very unlikely to be true, however. I noted earlier that by any number of measures the institutional quality of states in East Asia was higher than that of their counterparts in

Latin America, which was an important factor explaining their superior economic performance. But what happens when Japanese or Korean-style economic planning agencies are transplanted to Brazil or Pakistan?

A moment's reflection should make it obvious that the development of formal institutions is strongly affected by cultural factors. The institutional quality of postwar economic planning agencies in Japan, Korea, and Taiwan did not emerge out of a technocratic how-to manual; it had its roots in a mandarin bureaucratic tradition specific to each country that stretched back for many centuries. The attitudes of the elites running those agencies had a huge impact on their ultimate success; the view that government office presents an opportunity for predatory rent-seeking is one that could have become widespread, but did not. The Weberian state had, in other words, historical precedents in Asian societies and was therefore much less susceptible to capture or undermining by neopatrimonialism or clientelism.

Another example of ways in which informal habits affect formal institutions concerns the role of social capital in a government's relations to its beneficiaries. Holding government agencies accountable to the public is to some extent a matter of institutional design and internal checks and balances, but ultimately, it is the people whom government supposedly serves who are responsible for monitoring its performance and demanding responsive behavior. Society organized into cohesive groups—whether in the form of parent-teacher associations (PTAs), watchdog groups, or advocacy organizations—is much more likely to demand and receive accountability than one consisting of disorganized individuals. On the other hand, civil society can degenerate into rent-seeking interest groups whose goal is not greater accountability but an increase in the scope of government subsidies or the substitution of government for civil society. Which of these outcomes prevails depends less on institutional design than on the nature of civil society itself.

Transferrable Knowledge about Institutions

The supply of institutions thus consists of at least four components, summarized in Table 1. It is fairly clear that the bulk of transferable knowledge lies in the first component—that is, in public administration and the design and management of individual organizations. At this micro-level, organizations can be revamped, destroyed, created anew, or managed for better or worse in ways that draw on the historical experience of a wide range of countries. To the extent that organization theory or a theory of public administration can be formalized, it can be transferred. I address how much formalization is possible in Chapter 2.

There is also some transferable knowledge in the second and third components—institutional design at the system level and, in particular, the design of viable democratic political systems. The founding of the United States of America between 1776 and 1789 was, in effect, just such an effort to create a democratic political system based on both theoretical design criteria and the institutional experience of other countries. The postwar constitutions of Germany and Japan sere also products of a conscious design effort.

The problem with this level is not that useful knowledge does not exist but rather that opportunities to actually apply it are infrequent. Countries are rarely refounded on a system-

Table 1. Components of instutitional capacity

Component	Discipline	Transferability
Organizational design and management	Management, public administration, economics	High
Institutional design	Political science, economics, law	Medium
Basis of legitimization	Political science	Medium to low
Social and cultural factors	Sociology, anthropology	Low

wide level, and once they are, path-dependencies (that is, the likelihood of remaining in a path due to the costliness of shifting from an existing set of institutions) take over and make it very difficult to make reforms (Krasner 1984). It often takes a crisis of one sort or another—whether external, like a war or pressure from foreign governments, or internal, like a revolution or economic collapse—to create the political conditions for major institutional reform.

The fourth supply-side component of stateness, norms and cultural values, can be manipulated by public policy only at the margin. Cultural values are indeed shaped by education, leadership, and interaction with other societies. They change over time. The quality of top-level economic technocrats in Latin America has grown enormously over the past generation, for example, as a result of their schooling in North America and Europe. They bring with them professional values regarding transparency and accountability that have spillover effects in their own countries. But the time necessary for society-wide change is long, and in the short run cultural values can be changed only on a micro-level—in individual organizations, schools, or villages.

The Demand for Institutions

I turn now from the supply of institutions to the demand for them. Institutional development and institutional reform will not take place in the absence of such demand. A joke told by economists has an economist and a student walking down the street when the student sees a hundred-dollar bill lying on the sidewalk in front of them. The student moves to pick it up, but the economist explains that the bill cannot possibly be there, because if it were, someone would have picked it up already (Olson 1996). Economists tend to believe, in other words, that if an incentive exists, it will automatically motivate behavior. The reality is that good economic institutions do not always generate their own demand. Even if the society as a whole is better off with good institutions, every new institutional arrangement produces winners and losers, and the latter can be depended on to protect their relative positions. In other cases, the problem may be cognitive: The society may not understand the relative efficiency or inefficiency of alternative institutions. This is the equivalent of not noticing the hundred dollar bill lying on the street.

In the field of political economy, a large amount of attention has been devoted in recent years to the conditions that would generate domestic demand for good institutions and policy reform. Much of this research has been done under the rubric of rational choice political science and operates under assumptions similar to those underlying rational optimization models of markets—that is, it assumes a stable institutional framework and voluntary bargaining over different institutional rules. Different political actors (land owners, labor unions, bureaucrats) come to the table with specific economic interests that are either helped or harmed by different institutional arrangements; game theory is often applied to understand different bargains that might be achieved to bring about reform (e.g., through side payments to losers). For example, North and Weingast (1989) explain the emergence of secure property rights in England after the Glorious Revolution of 1688 as a solution to the problem of credible commitment that was created through the exercise of arbitrary power by the Crown, a solution demanded by the winners of that revolution.

These explanations are often incomplete and unsatisfying because at virtually every historical juncture, game theory shows that there are usually a number of possible stable political equilibria. Many of these produce suboptimal institutional arrangements, and we are left begging the question of why demand for good institutions emerged at particular points in time. The answer is likely to depend heavily on unique historical circumstances. Greif (1993), for example, uses game theory to explain how the Maghribi traders in the eleventh century used multilateral coalitions to enforce contracts on agents in an environment where there was no overall political authority to provide a rule of law and how this system was more efficient than bilateral enforcement mechanisms. But the possibility of creating such a coalition depended heavily on a host of prior conditions, such as the fact that the Maghribi traders were part of a social network of Jews who had emigrated to North Africa from Baghdad. These traders socialized their members according to a "merchant's law" that served as a cultural, rather than contractual, ex ante means of behavior control. While the institution was rational, it arose historically out of a host of nonrational, contingent circumstances that could not easily be duplicated in other settings.

In other cases, it is not internal conflict that creates demand for institutions but rather a severe exogenous shock such as a currency crisis, recession, hyperinflation, revolution, or war. Tilly's (1975) classic explanation for the rise of the modern European nation-state argues that it was the need to wage war on an ever-larger scale that drove the demand for tax extraction, administrative capacity, and bureaucratic centralization in states like France, Spain, and Sweden. War and national security requirements have definitely been prominent sources of state-building in American history; intensive state-building occurred in the wake of the Civil War, the two World Wars, and the Cold War (Porter 1994).[4] There are certainly clear cases of this happening outside the West, such as Commodore Perry's black ships that led to the Meiji reforms in Japan, or

[4] A more recent case was the formation of the Department of Homeland Security—the first new cabinet-level department to be established in the United States since the 1970s—in response to the terrorist attacks of September 11.

Napoleon's entry into Egypt that led to the Ottoman reforms of the 1830s.

But Sorensen (2001) has pointed out that war has been a much less effective driver of state-building for the developing world than for Europe or Japan. The reasons for this are both complex and obscure. Sorensen suggests that later developers could simply acquire military technology off the shelf without having to undertake painful institutional reforms to properly utilize it. In addition, the post–World War II international system has stressed the sanctity of international borders and tried to enforce a no-conquest norm; under these conditions, the threat of national extinction as a result of war is less of a motivator for state-building.

The majority of cases of successful state-building and institutional reform have occurred when a society has generated strong domestic demand for institutions and then created them out of whole cloth, imported them from the outside, or adapted foreign models to local conditions. Early modern Europe; the United States after the American Revolution; Germany, Japan, and Turkey in the nineteenth century; South Korea and Taiwan in the 1960s; Chile; and New Zealand in the 1970s and 1980s were all such cases. If sufficient domestic demand exists, then supply usually follows, though the quality of that supply has varied from decade to decade.

Insufficient domestic demand for institutions or institutional reform is the single most important obstacle to institutional development in poor countries. Such demand when it emerges is usually the product of crisis or extraordinary circumstances that create no more than a brief window for reform. In the absence of strong domestic demand, demand for institutions must be generated externally. This can come from one of two sources. The first consists of the various conditions attached to structural adjustment, program, and project lending by external aid agencies, donors, or lenders. The second is the direct exercise of political power by outside authorities that have claimed the mantle of sovereignty in failed, collapsed, or occupied states.[5]

What we know about the techniques and prospects for generating demand for institutions from the outside is both extensive and discouraging. More than a generation's worth of experience with conditionality to bring about economic reform shows that it seldom works in the absence of substantial domestic demand for reform on the part of the country's elites, as was the case for brief periods with Argentina and Mexico. In the cases where there is no complementary domestic demand, conditionality has been a failure. Across the different countries of sub-Saharan Africa, for example, van de Walle (2001) shows that there is virtually no difference in the aid levels going to countries that have followed international advice on structural reform and those that have not. One repeatedly finds the same poorly performing states going back to the same aid trough time and time again, sometimes as the beneficiaries of debt restructuring and other times as beneficiaries of debt relief (Easterly 2001).

There are a number of reasons why conditionality has failed. One suggested by Easterly (2001) has to do with the structure of incentives on the side of the donor community. Donors and IFIs claim to want to help poor countries escape poverty, but the most poorly performing countries are likely to be the ones that fail to enact institutional and economic reforms, so enforcement of conditions means rewarding better-off countries that have succeeded in reforming. Exercising conditionality on bad performers means cutting off the poorest of the poor from external aid or finance. This kind of "tough love" may be theoretically defensible, but real-world donors don't like to give up the influence and power over client countries that dependence

---

[5] In the nineteenth century, these two forms of external pressure converged when European or American lenders would send gunboats to collect their loans.

brings and thus don't want to pull the trigger on these hapless countries. Moreover, the diversity of the international donor community ensures that if one particular donor actually does enforce conditionality, there will be another to step into its place. Even if conditionality could be enforced firmly, it is not clear that it would bring about serious reform. Holding on to a certain structure of political power is often a life-and-death issue for leaders of poor countries, and no degree of external public-goods financing from the donor community will be sufficient to offset losses of power and prestige that will accompany true reform.

The Bush administration took a different approach generating external incentives through its Millennium Challenge Account (MCA), in which grants will be offered in return for measurable improvement in performance by recipient countries. This approach to conditionality differs from past efforts by using concessional assistance rather than loans and by using broader, countrywide indicators. The problem with the MCA is that the criteria used to judge country eligibility mean that many of the world's poorest countries will not begin to qualify for grants anytime soon. The MCA may stimulate countries well on the road to reform, but it will do little for failed states and the world's more troubled countries.

The other external source for creating demand for institutions is the political power exercised directly by countries or consortia of countries as occupation authorities or through a strong direct relationship with the local government. This is what we label "nation-building." An occupation authority obviously has much more direct leverage over the local country than does an external lender or aid agency working through conditionality. On the other hand, most nation-builders soon find that their ability to shape the local society is very limited as well. Moreover, most countries in need of nation-building are failed states or other types of postconflict societies with far more severe governance problems than the average recipient of a conditional loan.

If nation-building means the creation of self-sustaining state capacity that can survive once foreign advice and support are withdrawn, then the number of historical cases where this has happened successfully drops to a depressingly small handful. The most notable examples come from the history of European colonialism. The British above all succeeded in creating durable institutions in a number of their colonies, such as the Indian civil service and the legal systems in Singapore and Hong Kong that are widely credited as laying the basis for postindependence democracy in the first case and economic growth in the latter two. The Japanese as well left behind some durable institutions during their colonial period in Taiwan and Korea; despite the hatred of many Koreans for Japan, South Korea has sought to recreate many Japanese institutions, from industrial combines to one-party government.

The United States is sometimes credited with successful nation-building in postwar Germany and Japan, where it was an occupying power. In terms of the administrative capacity that is the subject of this book, it is clear that nothing of the sort happened. Both Germany and Japan were both very strong bureaucratic states long before the United States defeated them; indeed, it was the strength of their states that led them to be great powers and threats to the international system in the first place. In both countries, the state apparatus survived the war and was preserved into the postwar period with remarkably little change. What the United States did successfully was to change the basis of legitimation in both cases from authoritarianism to democracy and to purge members of the old regime that had started the war. The American occupation seriously underestimated the competence and cohesiveness of the Japanese bureaucracy and did little more than change a few positions at the top. In Germany, the postwar democratic government asked the allied occupation to permit them to keep in force a Nazi-era law governing their much-vaunted civil service. All but 1,000 of the 53,000 permanent civil servants initially purged were ultimately reinstated (Shefter 1993).

The United States has intervened and/or acted as an occupation authority in many other countries, including Cuba, the Philippines, Haiti, the Dominican Republic, Mexico, Panama, Nicaragua, South Korea, and South Vietnam (Boot 2003). In each of these countries it pursued what amounted to nation-building activities—holding elections, trying to stamp out warlords and corruption, and promoting economic development. South Korea was the only country to achieve long-term economic growth, which came about more through the Koreans' own efforts than those of the United States. Lasting institutions were few and far between.

Making Things Worse

There are thus grave limitations to the ability of external powers to create demand for institutions and therefore limitations on the ability to transfer existing knowledge about institutional construction and reform to developing countries. These limitations suggest that IFIs, international donors, and the NGO community more broadly should be cautious about raising expectations for the long-term effectiveness of its new "capacity-building" mantra.

But the problem is in fact even worse: The international community is not simply limited in the amount of capacity it can build; it is actually complicit in the *destruction* of institutional capacity in many developing countries. This capacity destruction occurs despite the best intentions of the donors and is the result of the contradictory objectives that international aid is meant to serve. That poor or collapsing public administration is at the heart of Africa's twenty-year development crisis is beyond doubt; since independence, the ability of

African governments to design and implement policies has deteriorated. In the words of the World Bank's African governors, "Almost every African country has witnessed a systematic retrogression in capacity in the last thirty years; the majority had better capacity at independence than they now possess" (quoted in van de Walle 2002). This deterioration in capacity has happened precisely during a period of accelerating external aid flows to the point where more than 10 percent of the GDP of the entire region comes from foreign assistance in various forms.

The contradiction in donor policy is that outside donors want both to increase the local government's capacity to provide a particular service like irrigation, public health, or primary education, *and* to actually provide those services to the end users. The latter objective almost always wins out because of the incentives facing the donors themselves. While many donors believe they can work toward both goals simultaneously, in practice the direct provision of services almost always undermines the local government's capacity to provide them once the aid program terminates.

For example, everyone would agree that a program designed to provide antiretroviral drugs to AIDS victims in sub-Saharan Africa would be desirable to implement. An outside donor has two possible approaches to treating victims. It can work entirely through the local country's public health infrastructure, expanding its reach by training bureaucrats, doctors, and other health care workers and providing the government with massively greater resources. Alternatively, it can take over important parts of the drug distribution program itself, directly providing doctors and other health care workers, drugs, and, most important, the administrative capacity to get the health care workers out into the field. Working through the local government inevitably means that fewer AIDS victims will be treated. The public health infrastructure may be nonexistent, incompetent, or highly corrupt; medicines will be stolen, records will not be kept, and donor funds will end up in the hands of bureaucrats rather than going to the patients they are meant to serve. Taking over these functions directly, by contrast, means a far more efficient delivery of health care services. But when the external aid agency bypasses the local government, the local government's function is less one of service provision than of liaison and coordination with the foreign donor. The local bureaucracy learns the wrong kind of skills, never takes ownership of the health care activity, and often sees many of its most skilled people leaving to work for the outside donor. The difference in resources available to the local government and to the outside donor is almost always enormous and means that the latter will often be marginalized in decision-making about the project's goals and implementation.

Notwithstanding efforts by IFIs like the World Bank to invite greater local participation in program design, the problem of capacity destruction cannot be fixed unless donors make a clear choice that capacity-building is their *primary* objective, rather than the services that the capacity is meant to provide. The incentives facing the majority of donors will usually not permit this to happen. Those footing the bill for aid programs want to see the maximum number of patients treated and do not want their money to go to local bureaucrats, even if it is these bureaucrats who must provide health care services in the long run. True emphasis on capacity-building is another form of "tough love" that, like conditionality, is very hard for well-intentioned people to actually carry out. So what we get in the meantime is lip service to the importance of capacity-building and the continued displacement of institutional capacity by outside donors.

As I discuss in Chapter 3, this problem does not go away but in fact becomes most severe when external leverage comes through nation-building rather than arms-length conditionality. The international community knows how to supply government services; what it knows much less well is how to create self-sustaining indigenous institutions.

It is true that governments in the developing world are often still too large and bloated in the scope of functions they seek to carry out. But what is most urgent for the majority of developing countries is to increase the basic strength of their state institutions to supply those core functions that only governments can provide. The problem of how to get to Denmark is one that probably cannot be solved, unfortunately, for quite a few countries. The obstacle is not a cognitive one: We know by and large how these countries differ from Denmark and what a Denmark-like solution would be. The problem is that we do not have the political means of arriving there because of insufficient local demand for reform.

For those countries that do have some prospect of getting at least part way to this promised land, we need to focus much more closely on those dimensions of stateness that can be manipulated and "built." This means concentrating on the public administration and institutional design components. We also need to focus particularly on the mechanisms for transferring knowledge about these components to countries with weak institutions. Policymakers in the development field should at least swear the oath of doctors to "do no harm" and not initiate programs that undermine or suck out institutional capacity in the name of building it. This topic constitutes the second chapter.

WEAK STATES AND THE BLACK HOLE OF
PUBLIC ADMINISTRATION

In Chapter 1 I argued that, of the different types of knowledge about institutions, that concerning the design and management of organizations was the most susceptible to formalization and hence to transferability across societal or cultural boundaries. In this chapter I argue that even within the limited domain of organizations, there is no optimal form of organization, both in the private sector and for public sector agencies. That there are no globally valid rules for organizational design means that the field of public administration is necessarily more of an art than a science. Most good solutions to public administration problems, while having certain common features of institutional design, will not be clear-cut "best practices" because they will have to incorporate a great deal of context-specific information. This in turn has important policy implications for how we help strengthen states in developing countries and how we train practitioners in this field. Good solutions to public administration problems have to be, in some sense, local, which requires a very different relationship between governments in developing countries and their outside donors and advisors.

For all of its richness and complexity, a huge amount of organizational theory revolves around a single, central problem: that of *delegated discretion*. The conundrum of organizational theory is that while efficiency requires the delegation of discretion in decision making and authority, the very act of delegation creates problems of control and supervision. In the words of one leading organizational theorist:

> Because all information cannot be moved to a central decision maker, whether a central planner in an economy or the CEO in a firm, most decision rights must be delegated to those people who have the relevant information. The cost of moving information between people creates the necessity for decentralizing some decision rights in organizations and the economy. This decentralization in turn leads to systems to mitigate the control problem that results from the fact that self-interested people (with their own self-control problems) who exercise decision rights as agents on behalf of others will not behave as perfect agents. (Jensen 1998, 2)

The problem of delegated discretion underlies a host of issues in both economics and political science. It simultaneously explains the relative efficiency of markets over centralized planning in a macroeconomy (Hayek 1945) and the need for large corporations to adopt a decentralized, multidivisional structure (Chandler 1977). The problems of federalism and the relative merits of authoritarian versus democratic decision making are ultimately ones of delegated discretion. Thus the issues at the core of organizational theory have implications for the social sciences more broadly.

The idea that there is no optimal form of organization or a science of public administration will not come as news to longtime specialists in the fields of management or public administration. It may not be obvious, however, to those economists who have sought to import their powerful methodological tools into the study of governance and institutions. There was a period when economists saw firms and organizations as "black boxes"—that is, actors whose external behavior was explainable through the normal assumptions of rational utility maximization but whose internal workings were largely closed to economic analysis. This view has given way in recent years to the attempt to incorporate organizations into broader economic theory, an effort that has yielded certain important and useful insights for public sector reform. In the end, the behavioral assumptions on which neoclassical economics rests—in particular, the assumption that people in organizations are motivated primarily by individual self-interest—are too limited to provide understanding of key aspects of organizational behavior. Economics as a science likes to generate theories that produce optimizing solutions, which is precisely what is not possible in many aspects of public administration. The black box indeed may resemble more of a black hole from the standpoint of theory.

The domination of the field of organizational theory by economists in the 1980s and 1990s has eclipsed an earlier sociological vein of theory about organizations and has obscured some of the major insights of that tradition. This change represents, in effect, regression in the social sciences. Some economists, recognizing the limitations of their approach, are now returning to these earlier theories and trying to restate them in terms of their own methodological assumptions. They are in effect reinventing a forty- to fifty-year-old wheel, which they were responsible for forgetting how to use.

Institutional Economics and the Theory of Organizations

Economic theories about organizations[1] begin with Ronald Coase's (1937) theory of the firm, which established the basic

---

[1] For overviews of the intellectual history of the economists's approach to organizational theory, see Furubotn and Richter (1997, chapter 8) and Moe (1984).

distinction between markets and hierarchies and argued that certain resource allocation decisions were made within hierarchical organizations because of a need to economize on transaction costs. The costs of finding information about products and suppliers, negotiating contracts, monitoring performance, and litigating and enforcing contracts in decentralized markets often meant that it was more efficient to bring all of these activities within the boundaries of a single hierarchical organization that could make decisions on the basis of an authority relationship.

Coase's theory of the firm was actually not a theory *of* organizations but rather a theory of why the boundary between markets and organizations was drawn the way it was. Williamson (1975, 1985, 1993) used Coase's transaction cost framework and filled in many of the details about why hierarchies were used in preference to markets. According to Williamson, bounded rationality meant that parties to a contract could never fully anticipate all possible future contingencies and enact formal safeguards against possible forms of opportunism. Open-ended employment contracts and authority relationships permitted more flexible adjustment to unforeseen future states of the world. In addition, market efficiency rests on the existence of a large number of market participants in competition with one another. But large numbers tend to turn into small numbers in many specialized contracting situations, allowing contractors to take advantage of asymmetric information. Again, the solution was to bring these activities within the boundaries of the hierarchy through vertical integration.

Economics put its distinctive stamp on organizational theory, however, when it began to import its own individualistic behavioral assumptions inside the boundaries of the firm. Organizations are collections of individuals who manifest both cooperative and competitive or self-interested behavior. The earlier sociological approach to organizations often emphasized the cooperative aspect and used organic metaphors that spoke of organizations as if they were single organisms whose individual parts were all directed toward a common purpose. Coase's concept of hierarchy implied a similar unity of purpose arising through the authority relationship. Alchian and Demsetz (1972) by contrast argued that there was nothing unique about the authority relationship that differentiated it from voluntary relationships between market participants. Hierarchical firms could be understood as a nexus of contracts in which individual employees voluntarily agreed to accept hierarchical authority. There were limits to that acceptance; employees could decide to terminate the relationship within the conditions of the original labor contract at any time and looked to their individual self-interest in preference to accepting the firm's authority. The reason that hierarchical firms existed, according to Alchian and Demsetz, was because of the problem of monitoring joint output in which it was difficult to disentangle the relative contributions of a number of employees. Monitoring difficulties opened up the possibility for shirking and allowed organizational theory to incorporate the concept of adverse selection originally laid out by Akerlof (1970). That is, in a joint-output situation the individual worker has better information about his or her individual contribution than a third party, which could be manipulated to the worker's advantage. Controlling this shirking behavior through monitoring and incentives was argued to be easier in a firm than in an arms-length contracting relationship.

Virtually all subsequent economic theorists of organizations have accepted the view that organizations are simply bundles of individual labor contracts and that the behavior of an individual in a hierarchy can be explained by the same rational optimization strategies that characterize behavior in markets. Individuals cooperate in organizations, but only because it is in their self-interest to do so. The divergence between individual and organizational interests led to a major branch of theory under the heading of *principal-agent relationships* that is

Bureaucracy on the ground level

today the overarching framework for understanding governance problems.

Berle and Means (1932) recognized long ago that the divorce of ownership from management in modern corporations creates significant corporate governance problems. The owners, or principals, designate managers, or agents, to look after their interests, but the agents often respond to individual incentives that differ sharply from those of the principals. This is a problem with all forms of hierarchical organization and can exist at multiple levels of the hierarchy simultaneously. Jensen and Meckling (1976) introduced the concept of agency costs, which were the costs that principals had to pay to ensure that agents did their bidding. These costs included the costs of monitoring agent behavior and bonding the agent and the residual losses that occurred when the agent acted in ways contrary to the interests of the firm. Jensen and Meckling assumed that it was primarily the residual risk-bearers or owners who did the disciplining and on this basis developed a sophisticated theory of capital structure and its relationship to corporate governance. Fama (1980) argued, however, that the residual risk-bearers were not the only source of agent discipline. Managers or agents monitored and disciplined each other's behavior because agency relationships involved repeated interactions and there was a competitive market for managerial talent in which these evaluations would be important.

Once principal-agent theory had been articulated with regard to private firms, it was relatively simple to adapt the framework to explain public sector behavior (Rose-Ackerman 1979; Weingast and Moran 1983; Weingast 1984; Moe 1984; Harriss et al. 1995). In the private sector, the principals are the shareholders; corporate boards of directors are their agents, and members of senior management serve as agents of the boards. In the public sector, the principals are the public at large. In a democracy their first-level agents are their elected representatives; the legislators act as principals with regard to the executive branch agents delegated to carry out the policies they have legislated. Political corruption occurs when individual agents—government officials—put their own private pecuniary interests ahead of those of their principals. But agents can act contrary to principal wishes for other reasons as well, such as the desire to preserve their agencies and job security or from ideological motivations that differ with those for whom they nominally work.

Another major branch of contemporary economics, public choice theory, begins with the assumption that agents in public sector organizations will have very different agendas from those of their principals. (This is true even though public choice theory did not initially make explicit use of the principal-agent framework.) As elaborated by Tullock (1965) and Buchanan and Tollison (1972), public servants are no different from any other economic agent in seeking to maximize their individual self-interest. Rhetoric about "public service" implies that government officials will somehow be oriented toward acting in the broad public interest when in fact their behavior is better explained empirically by narrower self-interested motives.[2] The behavior of public officials can be influenced by bribes, campaign contributions, payoffs to family members, or promises of future employment. A great deal of private sector activity thus gets diverted from wealth-producing entrepreneurship to rent-seeking (Krueger 1974; Buchanan, Tullock, et al. 1980). The public choice perspective is ultimately pessimistic about the prospects for reshaping the motivations of government officials through norms.

A great deal of the work now being done to improve gover-

[2] One problem with the public choice framework is the question of what constitutes the self-interest of a bureaucrat or public official. In some versions of the theory, it is very narrow, having to do with salary, perquisites, and job security. But it is clear that bureaucratic self-interest is often interpreted much more broadly, in terms of serving the long-term interests of one's agency or in a long-term career path that is inevitably determined by institutional interests.

nance is therefore attempting to better align agent incentives with the interests of the principals. The general approach to aligning principal and agent interests is to promote greater transparency in the activities of the agents (a nice way of describing the monitoring of their behavior) and then to hold the agents accountable for their actions through the use of rewards and punishments. Much of the work of the public choice school is to devise constitutional and legal arrangements that minimize rent-seeking and other kinds of agency costs. Another approach—more workable in the private sector than for public agencies—is to reunite owners and managers by giving the agents stock options or other forms of equity ownership.[3]

Economic theories about organizations, like economic theories more generally, begin from a premise of methodological individualism. That is, organizations are fundamentally understood as collections of individuals who learn to cooperate socially for reasons of individual self-interest. This perspective thus tends to emphasize conflicts of interests between members of the group (that is after all what principal-agent problems are all about) and to underplay concepts like group identity, socialization, leadership, and so forth.

It is certainly worthwhile to try to understand problems of corporate governance or public corruption in principal-agent terms and to use this framework to design institutions that try to bring divergent incentives back into alignment. However, there are at least three basic reasons why there can be no optimal specification of formal institutions and thus no optimal form of organization, particularly for public sector agencies.

First, the goals of many organizations are unclear. Agents can carry out the will of principals only if the principals know

[3] This approach has a number of drawbacks, as evidenced by the corporate scandals of Enron, Worldcom, and other companies at the end of the technology bubble of the 1990s. Stock prices reflect too many factors, many of them not under the control of managers, to be an accurate measure of the management's individual efforts.

what they want the agents to do, but this is not always the case. Goals often emerge and evolve through complicated interactions between organizational players or are defined by the roles assigned to players in the organization—the so-called where you sit is where you stand rule (Allison 1971). Labor can be divided functionally in a variety of ways that necessarily favor one organizational goal over a another but never all simultaneously.

Second, formal systems of monitoring and accountability, particularly in public administration, either entail very high transaction costs or are simply impossible because of the lack of specificity of the underlying activity. In these cases it is often more efficient to control agent behavior through informal norms, but control of agent behavior through norms has its drawbacks as well. An organization's choice of formal or informal control mechanisms will depend on the particular circumstances it faces.

Third, the appropriate degree of delegated discretion will vary according to the endogenous and exogenous conditions that an organization faces over time. All delegation involves a tradeoff between efficiency and risk, and both the degree of risk and the appropriate level of delegation are often difficult for organizations to determine. The result is that the same degree of delegation will work in one setting and not another or in one time period and not another. I consider each of these points in turn.

The Ambiguity of Goals

The first source of organizational ambiguity is that organizational goals are often unclear, contradictory, or otherwise poorly specified. The principal-agent framework assumes that principals are rational actors who understand their own self-interest completely and delegate authority to agents in pursuit of those interests. Authority flows in one direction, from the top of the hierarchy down. Problems like corporate malfeasance, corruption, or even simple bureaucratic inertia then occur as a result of self-interested behavior on the part of the agent, who does not face the same incentive structure as the principal or who misunderstands or fails to obey the principal's authority.

But there has long been a major branch of organizational theory that has emphasized the limited rationality of organizational participants, including the principals who supposedly use their authority to set organizational goals. The most notable example is Herbert Simon's concept of "satisficing," which he articulated in his book *Administrative Behavior* (1957) to explain how the empirically observed behavior of individuals in organizations deviated from the economic model of rational optimization. Other works in this tradition include Cyert and March (1963), Olsen and March (1976), March and Cohen (1974), and Cohen, March, et al. (1972). These theorists argue that goals never exist clearly at any given time but rather emerge as the result of interactions among different organizational players. These players have bounded rationality, not in Williamson's sense of not being able to accurately predict future states of the world but because the observation and interpretation of events is itself a social process that colors, distorts, and changes the cognitive process. Individuals learn, but organizations also learn in ways that are different from the sum total of individual learning: They have their own myths, histories, and traditions that shape individual perception. This view of knowledge as socially embedded anticipates in many ways newer studies about the effects of networks on organizational learning (Brown and Duguid 2000).

One of the drawbacks of the principal-agent framework is its assumption that authority flows in one direction: downward. Many of the conflicts that occur between principals and agents are the result of differing interpretations of how best to achieve common goals in which the principal may not always be right or in which there are conflicting interpretations of what constitutes the principal's best interests. Simon, Smithberg et al. (1961) long ago noted that authority flows not just top down but also bottom up and laterally within organizations—that is, different parts of an organization embed different forms of expertise or knowledge, like accounting, engineering, marketing, or human resource management. Specialization and the division of labor require that members of the organization defer not just to sources of authority higher than themselves in the hierarchy but also to the authority of possessors of these specialized forms of knowledge. Indeed, many organizations have formal rules requiring deference to certain specialists: A CEO cannot simply overrule the authority of the accounting department and demand that an expense be classified a certain way. The complex structure of authority within an organization thus explains why they are frequently so conservative, hard to move, and indeed "bureaucratic."

A significant proportion of the conflicts and dysfunction that exist in organizations concern precisely this kind of disagreement over authority or, as it is more commonly termed, "turf." A school administrator wants to improve test scores by hiring innovative nonunionized teachers; the teachers union responds by saying that the newcomers do not have the professional credentials to teach and that teachers as a corporate body should control who gets hired. Both the administrator and the teachers are acting as agents for the parents and children who consume the school's educational output and are thus the principals. Which agent's interests are misaligned with those of the principals? Perhaps it is the teachers, who want to protect their jobs and privileges, but maybe it is the administrator, who wants to get his unqualified brother hired as a teacher. In this case, the authority of the teachers as a professional group protects the principal's interests. The authority of teachers over the hiring process originated, after all, as a type of formal control over the discretionary behavior of administrators and not simply as a concession to the teachers's political power. All agents are claiming to speak on behalf of the interests of the principals; it is impossible to know in advance which is correct and impossible to specify a formal structure of authority that will guarantee a proper outcome.

Within any complex organization—indeed, within modern societies more generally—authority is necessarily distributed functionally, which is the origin of what pejoratively are known as "stovepipes." Stovepipes exist because they embed genuine knowledge and expertise. For example, within the Navy, aviators do a very different activity from submariners and surface warfare specialists. But each stovepipe develops a corporate interest in its own survival that may not reflect the interests of the larger entity of which it is a part. The Navy and Army both resisted the creation of an independent Air Force at the time of the National Security Act of 1948 (Quester 1973); pilots within the Air Force today resist the growth of a branch operating remotely piloted vehicles (RPVs). Agent interests become misaligned over time because of changes in technology and external circumstances. Disagreements often reflect genuine cognitive uncertainties over what constitutes the best interests of the principals. Today, highly trained pilots of combat aircraft argue that too much emphasis on RPVs will lead to a deterioration of pilot skills that will be critical in future wars. They are certainly promoting their own interests by making this case, but for all we know today, they may be right about the nature of future wars.

There are other sources of organizational ambiguity that ensure that no particular formal specification of an organization will ever fully optimize the organization's goals. The division of labor and the assignment of people to tasks will affect the organization's overall goals. Simon, Smithburg et al. (1961, 151) point out that labor can be divided functionally by purpose, process, client group, and geographical area. Organizations will emphasize different goals depending on which function is subordinated to which (e.g., whether the primary division is geographical and the secondary one process-related, or vice versa). Organizations have tried to get around these problems through techniques like matrix management and ad hoc project-based organization, but none of these solves the fundamental problem of embedded priorities. While some labor assignment problems are susceptible to mathematical optimization, others are not because they involve tradeoffs between goals whose relative utility is indeterminate or politically determined.

How will agents be monitored?

Principals, Agents, and Incentives

Agent incentives can never be fully aligned with the interests of their principals. A great deal of organizational theory concerns mechanisms to bring these incentives into greater alignment. It is impossible, in many circumstances, to monitor the outputs of agents in ways that permit them to be held accountable for their actions. An alternative method for controlling agents makes use of norms and the active shaping of the agents's utility functions. The ability of these two approaches to complement each other and be substituted for each other constitutes the second source of organizational ambiguity.

Monitoring agent behavior and holding agents accountable is particularly difficult in the public sector. Public sector organizations produce primarily services, and service sector productivity is inherently hard to measure. The problem of monitoring and accountability is bad enough in private sector organizations, where there are at least profitability benchmarks for measuring output, but it becomes virtually impossible to solve for many types of public sector outputs. If the latter cannot be measured accurately, there can ultimately be no formal mechanism for delivering transparency and accountability.

To illustrate this point I will borrow a framework developed by Woolcock and Pritchett (2002) in a brilliant paper on public sector reform but modified slightly using categories developed by Israel (1987). Woolcock and Pritchett distinguish between two aspects of public sector services: their transaction intensity and their discretionary character. The former refers to the number of decisions that need to be made by organizations, which can range from very small (e.g., decisions to change interest rates at a central bank) to very large (taking in deposits in a retail banking system or delivering primary education). *Discretionary* refers to a decision that requires a judgment of imperfect or incomplete information by a skilled decision maker, as opposed to one that can be routinized. Central banking, by this measure, is highly discretionary; retail commercial banking is not.

In place of discretion, I propose to substitute the category of specificity developed by Israel. *Specificity* refers to the ability to monitor a service output. The example he gives of a highly specific service is jet aircraft maintenance, a complex skill that is hard to fake. If a mechanic is incompetent, there will be immediate consequences. By contrast, high school guidance counseling is a service with very low specificity. The counselor may advise a student to change career directions; the advice may not be taken immediately, and, even if it is, its impact on the student's later life may not be known for years (if at all, since measurement requires a counterfactual comparison). This is not to say that the counselor does not perform an important function that can be done better or worse; it is simply one that cannot be measured easily.

We can thus set up a matrix that arrays transaction intensity against specificity, as in Figure 9. This again yields four quadrants, each of which poses a different problem of monitorability. The most easily monitored activities are those in quadrant I, which are both highly specific and low in transaction volume. An example would be a general conducting a military

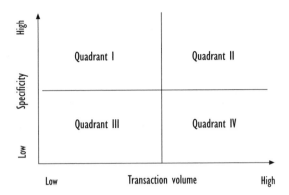

Figure 9. Public sector outputs.

campaign: His transactions are few in number and highly specific; if he fails, everyone will know it. The least able to be monitored are those in quadrant IV, which are characterized by low specificity and high transaction volume. Activities in quadrant II have higher transaction volume but also higher specificity; running a state-owned telecommunications company would be an example. Quadrant III is probably the least populated; an example might be running a foreign ministry in periods of relative international calm. The volume of decisions made by a foreign minister is low, but their impact on a country's well-being can often be hard to interpret. Quadrants II and III therefore constitute intermediate categories with different types of monitoring problems. Other public sector activities can be located in different parts of the matrix as in Figure 10.

It is not surprising that the most problematic areas of public administration are those falling in quadrant IV. There are many developing countries today, such as Mexico or Argentina, that have or have had highly competent central banks and can operate a national oil company or airline with reasonable competence but that have poor primary education or rural health care systems. Telecommunications companies have higher speci-

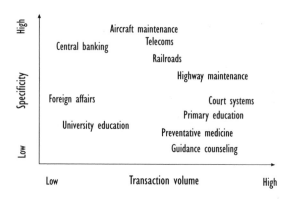

Figure 10. The ability to monitor public sector outputs.

ficity than do highway maintenance organizations or railroads, which probably explains why telephones often work better in the same country than highways (Israel 1989). University education has a much lower transaction volume than primary education. Thus, there are countries that operate successful elite institutions in large cities, where their middle class clients are much better able to monitor their output than the more diverse clients of the primary school system.

If one regards the central problem of public administration as that of creating a formal institutional system that aligns agent interests with those of the principals, then the hardest cases will all be in quadrant IV. Primary and secondary public education are clear examples. Educational outputs are hard to measure, and it is virtually impossible to hold individual teachers accountable. Public education is a high transaction volume activity that can be very visible in capital cities but out of sight in rural areas. Even in a wealthy and data-rich country like the United States, it has been very difficult to develop accountability mechanisms. Much of the drive for standardized testing in many states seeks to meet this need, but it is fiercely resisted by teachers and school administrators and by local communities that do not want to deal with the consequences of low performance.

Many people speak of the "rule of law" as if it were a binary condition that is either on or off. In fact, legal systems are medium- to low-specificity activities with high transaction volumes. Establishing a rule of law involves extensive construction not just of laws but also of courts, judges, a bar, and enforcement mechanisms across the entire country. Putting such a system in place is one of the most complex administrative tasks that state-builders need to accomplish.

There are a number of possible approaches to the problem of monitoring low-specificity activities with high transaction volume. One that is usually not available to public sector organizations is competition, or what Hirschman (1970) labeled the "exit" option. Private firms compete against each other and face the possibility of either gaining more resources or going out of business. The drive toward privatization of public sector activities like state-owned airlines, telecommunication companies, or oil companies is designed to subject these enterprises to competitive pressures. There are other public services with high transaction volume like education that can be subjected to similar competitive pressures through vouchers or, if they are to be kept within the public sector, charter schools, but market-based solutions to public sector dysfunction are very controversial and not politically possible in most jurisdictions.

The remaining alternatives are what Hirschman calls "voice" options, which seek to give principals better access to information about agent behavior and mechanisms for holding the agents responsible. Much of the emphasis on federalism, decentralization, and the nongovernmental organization (NGO) sector in recent years falls in this category—that is, political power over public institutions is moved to local communities that are directly affected by them. A local PTA should in theory be able to hold a local public school accountable to a greater degree than a national organization overseeing a national educational system. In this case, both the information available to the principals and their incentive for demanding accountability are greater for the local organization than the national one.

There are several limitations to this approach, however, which effectively prevent the emergence of significant "voice" in public agencies, particularly those in quadrant IV. The first is that decentralization addresses only the transaction volume problem by putting local principals in touch with local agents. It does not solve the specificity problem, which has to do with the inherent difficulty in evaluating the underlying activity. Moreover, the principals themselves have to be organized, which explains much of the recent interest in civil society and the NGO sector. Such organization cannot be taken for granted and is usually not something that can be brought about through public policy. Finally, many public sector organizations have independent bases of political power. Even if parents are organized into PTAs and are armed with plentiful information on the performance of their local schools, they may not have the political power to sanction poorly performing teachers or administrators or to reward good ones.

Many organizations do not "solve" the principal-agent problem through a formal system of monitoring and accountability at all. Rather, they rely on a mixture of formal mechanisms and informal norms, which usually is a more effective way of improving the quality of low-specificity outputs. Institutional economists have been trying to deal with the problem of "hidden action" for a long time (Miller 1992). In labor markets there are many activities where the individual output of a worker cannot be measured accurately. This has already been noted in the context of Alchian and Demsetz's discussion of joint labor but exists in other forms as well. A worker's output may be determined by various factors beyond his or her control (weather, exchange rates); the worker may have several tasks to which he can allocate his labor (Holmstrom and Milgrom 1991); or the output itself may be hard to measure. The latter is particularly true of complex services that a large literature on service sector productivity tells us is notoriously hard to measure (see, for example, Bosworth and Triplett 2000). Lawyers, doctors, architects, and other professionals all produce services that in many respects are of relatively low specificity. The principals who hire professionals as agents, for example, can usually detect instances of gross incompetence or fraud, but they have little way of judging the final quality of their agent's output relative to other possible outputs. An architect designs what looks like an acceptable house, but are there more creative variants she could have come up with that would have been more pleasing? Could she have done the same work in less time? The same is true of software engineering. Often the manager with nominal authority over a software engineer will be unable to read or evaluate the code produced. He will know whether it satisfies the minimal parameters of the task it is designed to perform but not whether it is as efficient or elegant as possible. The full qualities of the coder's work are thus very difficult to measure. (In some cases coders have been known to leave bombs or trapdoors in the code that only they know about.) The problem pointed to by organizational economists in all of these cases is shirking: Only the worker knows whether she has given full effort or whether she has gotten away with free riding of one sort or another. Economists have spent a great deal of time trying to devise incentive systems that would force workers to reveal their actual production functions; piece rates are one traditional way.

There is a certain blindness in this approach to the problem, however, that is caused by the basic behavioral assumptions underlying neoclassical economics. Economists posit that labor is costly and that workers will seek to minimize the amount of labor they will expend for a given wage. Indeed, they assume that workers will use their rational facilities to maximize the amount of shirking that they can get away with. The problem with this assumption is that many people do not shirk: They work more than is minimally necessary and do so even when they know that their boss has no way of monitoring their hidden action. Indeed, most workers probably work more than is called for in their labor contracts, since "working to rule" is a form of industrial protest used only on extraordinary occasions. Akerlof (1982) notes a situation in which young women working as cash posters for a utility worked 17.7 percent more than was called for by the company's standard. The Japanese lifetime employment/seniority wage system is almost deliberately designed to encourage shirking, since it removes the employer's ability to incentivize workers through wages, status, or the threat of dismissal. And yet, Japanese workers are famous for how hard they work. How does this happen?

Not just Japanese organizations, but organizations in all societies, seek to get optimal performance out of low-specificity activities not by setting up elaborate systems of monitoring and accountability and use of complex individual incentives but rather by relying on norms. Professionals in particular are motivated to do more than merely "satisfice" and maximize shirking. They perform against internalized standards of behavior that eliminate the need for their organizations to keep strict tabs on their behavior. Social capital—norms that promote cooperative behavior (Fukuyama 2000)—thus substitutes for elaborate formal incentive systems. Individual monetary incentives are always necessary as well, but only as a general motivator for performance.

Monitoring and strict accountability become more feasible in high-specificity activities like manufacturing. In a sense, Taylorism, or scientific management (Taylor 1911), represents the ultimate development of formal monitoring and oversight mechanisms to guarantee alignment of agent interests with those of principals. Taylorism is based on the systematic division of labor into small, simple tasks that are susceptible to a high degree of routinization. The system is highly hierarchical and segregates discretionary authority into the managerial layers. Workers in this system are motivated purely by positive and negative incentives and minutely regulated through administrative rules.

Taylorism produces a high level of transparency in agent output and total accountability of behavior. It is also a system of factory organization that requires no trust whatsoever between workers and managers. The monitoring required by Taylorism can also produce high agency costs, as well as excessive rigidity, hierarchy, and bureaucracy. For this reason, this form of factory organization has been increasingly displaced by flatter forms of organization like lean manufacturing that delegate a higher degree of discretion to employees at the bottom of the hierarchy. So even in manufacturing, there has been a tendency, undertaken purely in the interests of efficiency, toward a substitution of social capital for formal monitoring and accountability.

Social capital pervades organizations and is critical to their proper functioning. Individuals working within organizations have very complex utility functions that include individual economic interests, as well as commitments to group goals and values. On many occasions these group goals run counter to individual interests and often win out due to the very powerful natural emotions underlying human sociability (Fukuyama 1999). All formal organizations are overlaid with informal groups, which sometimes correspond to the formal organization's boundaries—whether agency, branch, division, or office—and sometimes cross these boundaries. All good managers know that it is ultimately the informal norms and group identities that will most strongly motivate the workers in an organization to do their best and thus spend much more time on cultivating the right "organizational culture" than on fixing the formal lines of authority.

The fact that a rule is internalized rather than being applied externally does not, of course, necessarily mean that it will be more strictly followed, or that shirking or opportunism aren't serious problems with norms. Informal norms work best when they supplement rather than replace formal incentive structures. Compliance with informal rules also needs to be monitored and failure to abide by them sanctioned. Informal norms have their own mechanisms for monitoring and enforcement, however, that can often be more subtle and flexible than formal mechanisms. Hidden action among members of a team may be hard for a supervisor to monitor, but it is not hidden to the team members themselves who have mechanisms like shaming and ostracism to keep shirkers in line.

The most extreme example of how public agencies can make use of norms and social capital is in military organizations. It is safe to say that normal individual economic incentives cannot motivate people to risk their lives in combat. Military organizations solve this problem not by increasing individual incentives but by replacing individual identities with group identities and reinforcing group identities through tradition, ceremony, and group experiences that are meant to bond soldiers emotionally. In U.S. Marine Corps basic training, trainees are not even allowed to refer to themselves by their given names, but simply accept the name "marine" (Ricks 1997). The strongest bonds are not to large organizations or abstract causes like the nation; rather they are to the immediate group of soldiers in one's platoon or squad, before whom one would be ashamed to be a coward (Marshall 1947). Only through the repeated reinforcement of these group ties can individuals be made to overcome their natural fear of death.

Most public sector agencies do not, of course, require their members to risk death or make extraordinary sacrifices on behalf of the larger group. The best-run agencies are ones like the U.S. Forest Service under Gifford Pinchot, the Federal Food Agency under Harvey Wiley, or the FBI under J. Edgar Hoover that established very strong organizational cultures that motivated their workers to identify with organizational goals (Wilson 1989).

The importance of norms to organizations has the consequence of making a great deal of behavior within organizations indeterminate. *Homo economicus* was always recognized to be a caricature of how human beings actually behaved in the economic realm, but it was close enough to their actual behavior in markets to have predictive value. It is a much less reliable guide to behavior in organizations, since there is a much more complex balance of motivation between individual incentives and group norms and goals for members of organizations.

Moreover, while norms can be used to align agent incentives with those of the principals, they are a double-edged sword. Norms can embed the interests of the principal—for example, the commitment of teachers to providing the best possible education for their students—but they tend to take on a life of their own. Group identities and loyalties tend to crowd out consideration of other interests, including the interests of the organization to which a group is nominally subordinate. This is an alternative source of the stovepiping problem noted earlier, where a branch or division sees its own survival as more important than the goals of the parent organization. Norms are also sticky: People see loyalty to groups and group values as a good thing in their own right and are loathe to abandon them when they prove dysfunctional.

It should be noted that nothing I have written up to now explains why the problem of public sector performance is more severe in poor countries than in rich ones. It is always harder to produce good outputs for activities in quadrant IV than in quadrant I regardless of level of development. How is it then that *any* societies manage to provide decent public services in quadrant IV, or are at least relatively more successful than others?

One obvious answer has to do with resources: Poorly funded

poorly funded organizations function less well at all levels, so it is not surprising that public agencies in poor countries with poorly trained staff and inadequate infrastructure will have difficulties delivering services. However, there is another reason why low-specificity activities are performed more efficiently in developed rather than underdeveloped countries that has to do with norms. The kinds of internalized norms that motivate workers to do more than the minimum in exchange for their wages do not come naturally in any society; they are the result of education, training, and a socialization process that is partly specific to a particular profession and partly absorbed from the surrounding society. Modern societies multiply identities and thus the groups and norms to which individuals feel attached, which has the effect of weakening or diluting the sorts of primary relationships people naturally develop to family and friends. Modern societies place particular emphasis on professional or workplace identities and in their educational systems stress the need for these identities to override the primary ones. Workers, of course, can and do behave with a high degree of professionalism in developing countries, but their primary ties remain very strong, and the countervailing effects of socialization into the norms of the various professions is weaker, just as other forms of human capital are less developed. This reduces the possibilities for substituting social capital for formal monitoring and accountability, making the performance of low-specificity tasks less efficient. Those non-Western countries that have developed the most rapidly were the ones in East Asia that already had highly developed norms of professionalism in public service before they modernized.

Another factor may be at work. Norms in organizations can be learned through conventional education and training, but more often than not, they are inculcated from the top down by leadership. Leaders create norms not just by promulgating rules and regulations but also by the force of their example and personalities. In this sense, modern Weberian rational bureaucracies are actually not entirely Weberian and rational to the extent that they depend on nonrational norms and commitments and replicate themselves in some measure through charismatic leadership. On the other hand, they have also succeeded in routinizing the production of charismatic leadership, paradoxical as that may sound. (The routine production of charisma is not the same thing as Weber's concept of the routinization of charisma.) Strong institutions—the military services come to mind—emphasize the teaching of leadership as the core of their institutional identity.

In many developing countries, by contrast, production of leaders for modern Weberian-rational bureaucracies remains the province of the broader society. Leaders abound, but they often lead patronage networks that bring the norms of the surrounding society into the organization instead of creating a self-replicating system of leadership within the modern state.

Decentralization and Discretion

The third source of ambiguity in organizational design has to do not with *how* agents are controlled but the *degree* of discretion that they should be delegated at different levels of the hierarchy. There are some rules of thumb for the appropriate degree of decentralization that amount to something less than a formal theory. For example, the domain of responsibility granted to a particular level in a hierarchy should correspond to problems unique to its span of control. In politics, this is known as the principle of subsidiarity, in which decisions should be made by levels of government no higher than that necessary to perform a given function. A plant manager or program administrator, in other words, will appropriately make decisions relevant to his or her plant or program but is not in a position to make decisions about the appropriate allocation of resources between plants within a company or between programs in an international agency.

There are reasons to think that the functionally appropriate degree of delegation depends on technology and therefore changes over time. For example, many of the new technologies of the later nineteenth century, such as railroads, coal-powered energy sources, steel, and heavy manufacturing, benefited from extensive economies of scale and thus encouraged centralization.[4] By contrast, Malone, Yates et al. (1989), building on Coase's thesis about the relationship between transaction costs and hierarchy, have speculated that with the advent of inexpensive information technology, transaction costs would fall across the board and hierarchies would increasingly give way to either markets or to more decentralized forms of organization in which cooperating units did not stand in a hierarchical relationship to one another. Information technology creating lower transaction costs has provided the theoretical justification for many firms to flatten their managerial hierarchies, outsource, or "virtualize" their structures.

Long before the advent of the contemporary information revolution, Hayek (1945), following on von Mises (1981), pointed out that the growing technological complexity of modern economies dictated a higher degree of decentralized economic decision making. He noted that the vast majority of information used in an economy is local in nature, having to do with the specific conditions that are usually known only to local actors. Hayek argued that this explained the unworkability of socialist central planning under conditions of technological complexity: No planner could possibly assimilate and act on all of the local knowledge generated in a modern economy. It could be much better done by decentralized decision makers inter-

---

[4] Piore and Sabel (1984) have argued, however, that this was not a technologically necessary choice and that small-scale craft manufacturing could have survived in the twentieth century industrial environment.

acting in markets. The same consideration applies on the micro-level of organizations: The person most likely to know that there is a problem with the quality of a product from a supplier is likely to be the worker on the shop floor trying to bolt it on to a chassis rather than a vice-president sitting in corporate headquarters. Much of the organizational innovation in recent years that has led to practices like lean or just-in-time manufacturing and flat organizations is based on this insight—namely, that local agents need to be empowered to act on local knowledge, thereby avoiding all of the costs of moving information up and down hierarchies (Fukuyama 1999).

Moving the locus of decision-making authority down the hierarchy and closer to local sources of information also allows organizations to respond more rapidly to certain types of change in the external environment. This ability is particularly important if organizations are to adapt flexibly in periods of rapid technological change. When such changes are relatively small or subtle, a decentralized organization is often better able to adjust its behavior because the lower-level units are smaller and less committed to a certain way of doing business. Presumably innovation also will happen at a faster pace in a decentralized organization since the lower-level units are empowered to take risks and try new technologies or ways of doing business.

The need for delegated authority increases also when the work done by the agent is complex or involves a high degree of discretion and judgment. This is the case for service sector outputs involving the integration of a high level of skill with large amounts of context-dependent information, such as medicine, accounting, law, and so forth. These activities cannot be fully routinized in the Weberian sense or specified through formal rules and standard operating procedures. As an economy matures from industrial to postindustrial and increasingly depends on information and higher levels of worker skill, the degree of delegated discretion must also increase.

Similar considerations apply in politics as in organizations, under the heading of federalism. There has been a huge push within the development policy community since the 1980s to decentralize political authority to state and local government. The reasons are the same as for organizations: Decentralized decision making is closer to local sources of information and therefore inherently more responsive to local conditions and changes in the local environment. Decision making is quicker if it can be done locally, and when it is spread out over a large number of units, there can be competition and innovation among them (Wildavsky 1990). In addition, in politics, federalism means that government is closer and more visible to the people it is meant to serve, which theoretically should increase accountability and therefore the legitimacy and quality of democracy.

These kinds of considerations have led some observers to suggest that there is a long-term secular trend leading inevitably to higher degrees of decentralization and flatness in organizational structure. This trend is doubtful, however, because there are offsetting drawbacks to decentralized organizations that will never be susceptible to technical solutions. Decentralized organizations often generate high internal transaction costs and can be slower and less decisive than centralized ones. Thus, while military organizations typically delegate substantial local command authority to the lowest possible echelon, they nonetheless retain a high degree of centralized control over decisions at the strategic or operational level.

The most important drawback of decentralization concerns risk. Delegation of authority inevitably means delegation of risk taking to lower levels of the organization. It may be appropriate in areas like technological innovation, where constant low-level risk taking is always necessary, but in other cases, organizations can delegate undue authority to subordinate units that will affect the well-being of the firm as a whole. Sears

Roebuck, for example, went through a period of internal decentralization under CEO General Robert E. Wood when authority was granted to local stores during the 1950s and 1960s to set conditions for sales, marketing campaigns, and so forth. This decentralization continued until some local Sears auto service outlets in California engaged in a bait-and-switch operation that undermined the integrity of the Sears brand name (Miller 1992). In another example, the venerable British investment firm Barings delegated authority to, in effect, bet the company to a single young currency trader in Singapore, Nick Leeson. He then proceeded to make extremely large currency trades that undermined the capital structure of the company, forcing Barings into bankruptcy.

Federalism poses a similar problem. Delegation of authority to state and local government means almost inevitably there will be greater variance in government performance. Often variance is desirable, as when states engage in competitive experimental policy reform. In other cases, however, it means some subordinate units will fall below a minimum threshold of tolerability. The historical problem with American federalism, of course, was that it delegated to the states the authority to set rules on slavery, which, as Lincoln explained, undermined the basic principle of equality on which the country as a whole was founded.

In a more mundane fashion, the delegation of authority to state and local government in developing countries often means the empowerment of local elites or patronage networks that allows them to keep control over their own affairs, safe from external scrutiny. One of the chief reasons for recentralizing political authority is to ensure minimum standards of noncorrupt behavior in public administration. In Indonesia, the replacement of the authoritarian Suharto regime with a democratic one led to changes in the constitution that delegated more authority to provincial and local authority. The spreading out of authority simply increased opportunities for corruption (Richard Borsuk, "In Indonesia, of Power Multiplies Opportunities for Bribery, Corruption," *Wall Street Journal*, 30 Jan. 2003), which occurred not just at the top of the political hierarchy but throughout all of its echelons.

There are thus a host of complex technological and social factors bearing on the question of the appropriate degree of decentralization in organizations. In addition, issues of delegated authority are often approached not merely from a functional but also from a normative standpoint. In a tradition beginning with the French Revolution and continuing through the revolutions in Russia and China, political centralization was associated with modernity and progress. Today, decentralization is more often associated with higher levels of popular participation and control, and hence with positive values like democracy, and is desired as an end in itself.

There is a further important dimension of decentralization that makes it impossible to specify formally the optimal degree of decentralization in any given organization. It has to do with the nature of contextual judgment and the degree to which organizations need to trust subordinates to make certain kinds of decisions.

Modern constitutional government and the rule of law were established deliberately to limit discretion in the exercise of state power, as indicated by the phrase "government by laws and not by men" commonly attributed to Aristotle. But the rule of law by itself is not sufficient to achieve effective government; effective government requires discretion or, in the words of the Federalist papers, "energy in the executive." Hence rule-of-law states seek to reinsert carefully circumscribed domains of discretion back into executive power, particularly in areas like military command or monetary policy that combine technical expertise with the need for decisive action. The truth is that discretion is a necessary condition for the exercise of any type of authority and exists to some degree at virtually all levels of public administration.

The degree of discretion that an organization grants to a subordinate division, branch, office, or individual is among the most important institutional design decisions that can be made. The most effective organizations are inevitably those run by highly capable individuals who are granted a large amount of discretion and who face relatively few formal institutional controls. Good judgment is something that cannot be formalized, because it depends on weighing complex contextual factors against a background of experience that provides generalized models of human behavior. Economists refer to tacit knowledge that cannot be learned from a book but arises instead from a worker's active interaction with a piece of equipment. Such knowledge exists well beyond the factory floor and is part of the repertoire of capable presidents, program managers, CEOs, and administrators.

The fact that good judgment on the part of agents cannot be taken for granted is of course the reason that organizations cannot safely delegate large amounts of discretion. Since bad judgment is at least as likely as good judgment, organizations have to develop formal controls and standard operating procedures to constrain the discretion of the agents to whom authority is delegated. The degree of constraint should depend on the degree of risk to the organization's goals posed by discretion, but it is often driven by other exogenous factors. The reason that government procurement, for example, ends up being so costly relative to private sector procurement is that the public sector principals are willing to tolerate only miniscule degrees of risk in their delegation of authority. Fear that undue discretion will lead to corruption or abuse drives the proliferation of formal procurement rules (the Federal Acquisition Regulations) limiting discretion, without regard to the agency costs of such risk-averse policies. In addition, they load the decision process with other objectives like racial and gender equality or the promotion of small business, in ways that further constrain discretion.

In developed countries, the politically driven demand to limit the discretion of public sector agents is probably the biggest driver of the overly rigid and often irrational rules that people popularly associate with bureaucracy and big government. The fact that Zoë Baird hired an illegal alien as a nanny not only undermined her chances to be President Clinton's attorney general but also led to rules requiring all subsequent federal nominees to be scrutinized rigorously by the FBI for possible violations of employment laws in their hiring of nannies. In underdeveloped countries, the opposite situation may often apply, where the political system does not generate sufficient pressure to limit the discretion of bureaucrats. In these cases, the proliferation of further formal rules will serve to limit corruption, even if they drive up transaction costs.

The conceptual problem, however, is that there is simply no theory that can provide generalized guidelines for an appropriate level of discretion in public administration. The same degree of discretion will work well in some societies and not in others; within the same society, it can be functional at one time period but not in another.

An example is the industrial policies carried out by so-called developmental states like Japan, Korea, and Taiwan. Industrial policy involves government intervention to allocate credit and speed up the process of industrial development over what would have occurred had the process been left to free markets alone. It necessarily implies the delegation of a huge degree of discretion to the economic planning agencies managing it, which have the authority to "pick winners and losers" and in effect reward entire industrial sectors. In the hands of a competent, noncorrupt technocratic bureaucracy, industrial policy can be used effectively to compensate for the information inadequacies of underdeveloped capital markets. In the wrong hands, however, it can be used to steer investment resources to politically favored groups or indeed into the pockets of friends and family of those making the decisions.

As I noted in Chapter 1, economic planning ministries in several northeast Asian countries were notable for their relative competence, professionalism, and independence from rent-seeking societal interest groups. In the case of the Japanese finance ministry, the bureaucracy survived virtually intact from the wartime credit allocation system and continued to operate with relatively little outside scrutiny for the next generation (Sakakibara 1993; Hartcher 1998). An economic planning agency with the same formal specifications set up in, say, Brazil or Mexico would have produced very different results. The reasons for this would be various. The state in Latin America is not as autonomous as it was historically in Japan and would have been exposed to more societal pressures that would have sought to capture the credit allocation process. The quality of the bureaucracy would not have been similar because it would not have been fed by the same kinds of training institutions and traditions. And the willingness of parts of the underlying society to accept the authority of the state would have been different.

Even in the case of Japan, the same institution had different degrees of effectiveness at different times. The much celebrated historical autonomy of the finance ministry clearly began to deteriorate over time. By the 1980s, important parts of the ministry had been captured not just by individual sectors like the banking or savings and loan industries but also by influential factions within the ruling Liberal Democratic Party. In addition, its vaunted technocratic competence declined, as its disastrous management of the monetary bubble after the 1984 Plaza accord indicated (Hartcher 1998). These institutional weaknesses remain and explain to some extent the extended period of economic stagnation experienced by Japan starting in 1991.

Centralized and decentralized organizations thus have offsetting advantages and disadvantages. Which advantages prove decisive will depend on external conditions that cannot necessarily be known in advance. The best organizations are often those that are able to shift flexibly from one level of centralization to another in response to changing external conditions.

Losing, and Reinventing, the Wheel

The central problem that all organizations face is the delegation of discretion. The three sources of organizational ambiguity discussed above—limited rationality in setting organizational goals, alternative approaches to the control of agent behavior, and uncertainty as to how much discretion to delegate—are all related to this issue. Ambiguity implies that there are no theoretically optimal ways of specifying decision rights within an organization. Everything depends on context, past history, the identity of organizational players, and a host of other independent variables. Instead of equilibria or Pareto optimal solutions to organizational problems, there are continuous tradeoffs along a series of design dimensions.

The discipline of economics is characterized by a large body of abstract theory that postulates universal rules of human behavior. When applied to markets, that theory is robust enough to specify conditions of both equilibrium and optimality. It is also rigorously empirical and has clear standards for hypothesis testing and the use of data.

When the same methodological tools are used to analyze the inside of the black box of organizations, they yield useful and interesting results to the extent that people in organizations interact as self-interested individuals. But people in organizations interact differently than they do in the arms-length interactions characterizing markets: Norms, values, shared experience, and intense social relations at a variety of levels are much more present and actively shape the preferences or utility functions of the players.[5] For example, an employee joins a particular branch of an organization simply to have a job but then develops an intense loyalty to other members of her team, working nights and weekends to help the team defeat a rival. Another employee develops an intense dislike of a coworker and does everything he can to undermine that person even at the expense of the broader organization and his own career. A leader gives an inspiring speech about the higher aims of the organization that induces yet another employee to forego a higher-paying job at a different firm. While these kinds of a-rational motives appear in markets, they are much less common than in organizations.

The reason the study of management or public administration cannot be formalized to the extent of microeconomic theory is not because the field has yet to be approached with sufficient analytical rigor but because of reasons inherent in the subject matter. Organizations are pervaded by norms and other a-rational sources of behavior, which has important behavioral consequences. The reason that rationality is limited in an organizational context is because members of organizations perceive the world and calculate future outcomes through a social filter set by their coworkers. They substitute institutional judgment for individual judgment. They satisfice rather than optimize because their decision space is set by their social role or function. They are heavily motivated not simply by narrow economic self-interest but also by norms of loyalty, reciprocity, professional pride, or the desire to maintain tradition. Markets seldom shape individuals's sense of their own identity; organizations do.

---

[5] Modern economics has its own theory of norms, which emphasizes the ways decentralized individuals can rationally interact to generate norms that maximize their individual utilities (Ellickson 1991). The problem with this theory is that norms have many other nonrational sources, from tradition to religion to habit.

None of these insights are new. There is an older, more sociological tradition that put normative or moral issues at the forefront of theory about organizations. This tradition begins with Chester Barnard and his classic book *The Functions of the Executive* (1938).

Barnard wrote partially in response to Frederick Taylor and the mechanistic understanding of organizations that Taylorism promoted. Barnard agreed that organizations had to promote cooperation through rational systems of incentives, but a major part of his book deals with the informal norms of cooperation that exist side-by-side with the firm's formal structure. Where he differs most markedly from modern economists is in his view that preferences are not fixed but actively shaped by organizations and their leaders. In the words of Levitt and March (1990, 13),

> The Barnard strategy . . . include[s] conscious attention to the transformation of preferences. Changing motives is seen to be an important part of management, as is the creation of new moral codes. In modern terms, Barnard proposed that an executive create and sustain a culture of beliefs and values that would support cooperation. The appeal is not to exchanges, Pareto optimality, or the search for incentive schemes; it is to the construction of a moral order in which individual participants act in the name of the institution—not because it is in their self-interest to do so, but because they identify with the institution and are prepared to sacrifice some aspect of themselves for it.

Barnard also anticipated Simon's observations about limited rationality in organizations. He noted that behavior is structured around routines, which in turn were interpretations of the past rather than anticipations of future states of the world. The themes of limited rationality and the normative structure of organizations that first appear in Barnard were developed by a stream of later theorists that included Herbert Simon, Philip Selznick, Richard M. Cyert, James G. March, Michael Cohen, Edgar Schein, and James Q. Wilson. (Oliver Williamson might be included in this group, though much of his work seeks to incorporate organizational behavior into a broadened neoclassical economics framework.) I have already referred to Simon's concept of satisficing, but he was also insistent on the norm- and group-based nature of organizations as well. Chapters 4 and 5 of his classic work *Public Administration* (1961) focus on "The Formation of Groups" and "Group Values," respectively, and argue, à la Barnard, that public agencies actively shape the preferences of their workers.

The idea elaborated earlier that norms and cultural values serve as substitutes for formal monitoring-and-accountability systems has been a staple in this tradition. Simon and Smithburg (1961), for example, refer to both "bureau philosophy" (i.e., organizational or bureaucratic culture) and professional codes of behavior as varieties of informal controls over organizations that function in the absence of formal control. Philip Selznick, in his study of the Tennessee Valley Authority (1951, 50), makes the following observation:

> If a basic point of view is laid out and integrated into the psychology of the second and third level leadership, if not farther down the ranks, the possibilities of decentralization without injury to policy are vastly enhanced. It is almost axiomatic that in new organizations, in which the adherence of the administrative personnel to the viewpoint of the directorate is not dependable, measures of formal control from the top must be introduced. When, however, indoctrination of official policy has been sufficiently extended, formal controls may be loosened. Ideas and the attitudes they foster may serve as surrogates for a system of rules and formal discipline.

Delegation of discretion, in other words, is safer in conditions where agents share the same value framework as the principals, even in the absence of a formal monitoring and incentive structure. Selznick also follows Barnard in observing that organizations shape the preferences of their members: "The educational function common to all such structures of painlessly but effectively shaping the viewpoints of new members is facilitated, thus informally but effectively establishing the rubrics of thought and decision. This is well understood in practice, reflected in the use of organizational labels (a 'Forest Service' man, an 'agriculturalist,' etc.) so that special attitudes and characteristic administrative methods may be identified" (1951, 50).

Virtually every writer in this tradition has stressed the importance of leadership as a source of organizational culture. Norms and values come, of course, from the broader society and are influenced by components of social structure like class and ethnicity. But on the micro-level of organizations, norms can be actively shaped through the hierarchical structure of authority. Indeed, to many writers in this tradition the normative function of hierarchy is often more important than its formal powers. As Selznick argues in his book *Leadership in Administration* (1957, 27–28), "the role of the institutional leader should be clearly distinguished from that of the 'interpersonal' leader. . . . His main contribution is to the efficiency of the enterprise. The institutional leader, on the other hand, *is primarily an expert in the promotion and protection of values.*"

The Barnard-Simon-March line of theorizing about organizations has been eclipsed by the institutional economics framework. One of the reasons for this change was that the earlier approach did not lend itself readily to the kind of formal modeling preferred by economists. By relaxing assumptions about rationality and adding altruistic or social preferences to individual utility functions, human behavior in organizations becomes increasingly indeterminate. Indeed, writers like Cyert,

March, and Cohen often end up being more descriptive and taxonomic in their discussion of organizations than truly theoretical. The economists reset these assumptions back to simpler states where individuals were assumed to be rational and utility functions more narrowly self-interested. This restored the possibility of mathematization and predictive theory but at the cost of reductionism and lack of realism in the starting assumptions. Thus did organizational theory become yet another battlefield in the broader methodological struggle taking place across the social sciences.

It is possible to overstate the differences between the older sociological and later institutional economics approaches to theory about organizations. Barnard and his followers thought seriously about incentives and the formal structure of organizations. Conversely, institutional economists recognize the importance and functions of norms and culture in organizations and the way that norms can both supplement and substitute for formal incentives. Akerlof (1982), as noted earlier, describes workers following a norm of service to one another, which he understands, being an economist, as a form of gift exchange. The difference is more one of emphasis: The economists tend to spend most of their time modeling the incentive structure of an organization and devising complex strategies for optimizing it, while the older school spent much more time elaborating strategies for shaping the normative environment. It is safe to say that relatively few economists have spent time writing in the manner of Schein (1988) about the role of leadership in organizations, how leaders are trained, and how they communicate and inspire workers. One exception is Gary Miller in his book *Managerial Dilemmas* (1992, 217), who concludes that leaders "shape expectations among subordinates about cooperation among employees, and between employees and their hierarchical superiors. This is done through a set of activities that have traditionally been in the realm of politics rather than economics: communication, exhortation, symbolic position taking." Miller was, alas, reinventing a wheel that had been first rolled out over fifty years previously. Such is the nature of progress in the social sciences.

Capacity-Building under Conditions of Organizational Ambiguity: Policy Implications

A number of important practical implications flow from the theoretical conclusion that there are no optimal organizations. The first is to support the conclusion of Woolcock and Pritchett (1992) that in development policy, we have to be very careful about asserting the existence of broadly applicable rules or lessons that can be applied to public sector reform, project management, or service delivery. They emphasize the frequently dysfunctional character of "best practice" mentality, where a practice that works in one part of the world is immediately publicized and set up as a model for other parts of the world to follow. Successful programs are often idiosyncratic, involving what James Scott (1998) labels *metis*—the ability to use local knowledge to create local solutions.

The importance and pervasiveness of norms in management and public administration imply that institutional development will be heavily impacted by social structure, culture, and other variables not under the direct control of public policy. Organizations create and foster norms through socialization and training, but norms also spill over from the surrounding society. If obligations to kin inevitably trump obligations to strangers despite legal or contractual ties, then certain types of administrative dysfunctions will be inevitable regardless of the formal institutional controls put in place to control corruption.

It should not be surprising that public administration is idiosyncratic and not subject to broad generalization. After all, Hayek's observation that most knowledge in an economy is local has been taken to heart and embedded in our preference for decentralized, market-based economic systems. Why should we permit—indeed, encourage—a high degree of diversity in the way that private firms organize themselves and make business decisions and yet insist that public agencies be stamped out of a single, best-practice administrative die?

The great disadvantage of public administration compared to private sector management is that private firms are exposed to a ruthless Darwinian process of competition and selection, while public sector agencies are not. Armen Alchian, in his classic article "Uncertainty, Evolution, and Economic Theory" (1950), pointed out that random variance in firm strategies and organization would be sufficient to produce evolution toward efficiency over time as less efficient firms were weeded out. In the public sector, comparable worst-practice sanctions don't exist, so that highly suboptimal administrative arrangements can remain in place for long periods of time. Hence the need for rational foresight and consideration of alternative administrative models.

The fact that organizational ambiguity exists does not mean that we throw up our hands and assert that "anything goes" in public administration. While there may not be best practices, there are certainly worst practices, or at any rate bad practices to be avoided. The broad thrust of institutional economics to model and optimize formal incentive structures is not wrong and in fact is very useful for uncovering and reforming broken or dysfunctional incentive systems. The problem with this approach is only that it is incomplete as a solution for organizational dysfunction. An excessive emphasis on norms, or over-punctilious deference to local customs and traditions, can leave in place highly counterproductive incentive structures that could be readily fixable through public policy.

Of the different components of institutional capacity, public administration is the one that is the most susceptible to systemization and transfer. The existence of public administration schools all over the world is testimony to this fact. The kinds of institutional reforms and changes in formal incentive structures that have brought about more professional and less corrupt government in the United States, Great Britain, and other developed countries can also be applied quite successfully in developing countries as well.

This success, then, suggests a research agenda. We need to understand better which types of public sector activities are most susceptible to formal modeling and analysis and conversely which ones are likely to see a high degree of local variance. The matrix laid out in Figure 10 is a starting point. There are some high-specificity activities with low transaction volume like central banking that do not permit a high degree of variance in institutional structure and approach. These are the areas of public administration most susceptible to technocratic reform, where (to use the Woolcock-Pritchett language) "ten bright technocrats" can be air-dropped into a developing country and bring about massive changes for the better in public policy. And indeed this has happened over the past couple of decades in a series of countries including Chile, Bolivia, Argentina, and Mexico.

By contrast, the hardest areas to reform are the low-specificity activities with high transaction volume like education or law. There is no legal system in the world that can be "fixed" by ten technocrats, no matter how bright. These are also the areas of public administration that are likely to be the most idiosyncratic and subject to variance according to local conditions. These are areas where design and input from people immersed in local conditions will be the most critical. In these cases each transaction may have to be different, in some sense, to take account of ethnic, regional, religious, and other types of diversity within a society. Woolcock and Pritchett, recognizing the complexity and diversity of possible good solutions, suggest that the most successful project managers are ones who have been granted a high degree of discretion and have been in the field for long enough to understand the subtleties of the local environment.

The most difficult cases are the ones in the middle of the matrix, of moderate specificity and transaction volume, that will be susceptible to best-practice design to a limited degree. Here the problem is that outsiders to a society may be tempted to think that they know more than they actually do about the universality of a particular institution or practice. Take the question of civil service reform and personnel systems. Elimination of patronage was the key to administrative capacity-building in developed countries like Britain and the United States and came about through major reform efforts like the Peel Reforms and the Hatch Act. Public bureaucracies in developing countries are riddled with patronage and corruption, and cleaning them up through the implementation of "modern" civil service systems has been a central goal of institutional reform.

Even in this domain, there are a variety of ways of skinning the cat. Across the developed world, "modern" bureaucracies exhibit considerable variance in the way they recruit, train, promote, and discipline civil servants. The "mandarin" systems that exist in Japan and France are quite different from the approach taken in the United States and allow the Japanese and French bureaucracies to undertake activities that would be difficult to carry out in the United States. Blindness to these differences has led to important policy failures in the past.

When the United States arrived in Japan in late 1945 as an occupying power, it embarked on a much-celebrated "nation-building" exercise to turn Japan into a democracy. The Japanese imported many Western institutions, including a new constitution that was written by General MacArthur's staff, with surprising success (see Dower 1999). In other areas, American approaches to institutional reform did not take. The U.S. effort to dismantle Japan's industrial conglomerates or *zaibatsu* simply prompted the re-emergence of these institutions in the form of the *keiretsu* in the following decade. The most striking failure was in the American effort to reform the Japanese bureaucracy, a job undertaken by a U.S. official named Blaine Hoover. Theodore Cohen, who served as Labor Commissioner on MacArthur's staff, provided the following account of Hoover's mission (1987, 381):

> The chairman of the new mission . . . was Blaine Hoover, president of the prestigious Civil Service Assembly of the United States and Canada . . . A lifetime of personnel administration within the US federal civil service system was the basis, if not the sum, of their expertise.
>
> On its arrival in Japan in November 1946, the mission launched itself into a comprehensive series of familiarization briefings by the appropriate SCAP agencies . . . it seemed to me that members were screening what I said, absorbing factual data they thought usable but rejecting information that did not fit their preconceptions. When I tried to explain the Japanese employer-employee relationship as an exchange of protection for loyalty, not money for work, their eyes glazed over. When I talked of the network of patron-client (oyabun-kobun) relationships that pervaded all large Japanese organizations, including the government bureaucracy, it drew no follow-up questions. To me that was the central problem of "defeudalizing" the kanbatsu bureaucracy. . . . But the mission men were more interested in a comparison of governmental and private wage scales. They had no room in their mental baggage for the psychology and attitudes of the people for whom they had been called upon to prescribe their modern, scientific, nonfeudal administrative system.
>
> Instead, they used purely American concepts of equal opportunity for promotions and fair play for civil service workers, or the noble idea of service to the public.

Hoover delivered an indictment of the seven deadly sins that had affected the Japanese administration system: overstaffing, inefficiency, poor discipline, poor training, ineffective employee evaluation and utilization, classification based on civil service rank rather than duties and employment, and examinations testing general rather than specialized knowledge. Unsurprisingly, his prescription turned out to be in the main equally conventional, a compound of merit examinations, "scientific" job descriptions, wage classifications, efficiency ratings, plus an independent civil service authority. What had all this to do with feudalism? An American arrangement designed historically to eliminate the spoils system was to be applied to a country that had none. I sometimes thought that if the Mission had been sent to the Artic Circle instead, it would have come up with the same prescription for the Eskimos, seals, and seagulls.

It is hard to know which was more striking—the Hoover mission's ignorance of local conditions or its arrogance. In retrospect, the Japanese bureaucracy in 1946 was in many respects more elite, competent, and shielded from demands for political patronage than its American counterpart at the time. The U.S. reformers failed to remove any but the very top levels of the existing administration and left in place a machinery that evolved in a very short period into agencies like the much-feared Finance Ministry and Ministry of International Trade and Industry that tormented Americans during the trade wars of subsequent decades.

The local character of the knowledge required to design a wide variety of good administrative practices suggests that administrative capacity isn't actually transferred from one society to another by developed-world administrators sitting around lecturing their less-developed counterparts about how things are done in their country or in a mythical "Denmark." General knowledge of foreign administrative practices need to be combined with a deep understanding of local constraints, opportunities, habits, norms, and conditions. This means that administrative and institutional solutions need to be developed not just *with* input or buy-in from the local officials who will be running local institutions, but *by* them. The East Asian fast developers with strong governance imported certain institutions but modified them substantially to make them work in *their* societies. They certainly did not grow by allowing foreign donors to establish institutions in their own country that crowded out domestic ones.

If we really want to increase the institutional capacity of a less-developed country, we need to change the metaphor that describes what we hope to do. We are not arriving in the country with girders, bricks, cranes, and construction blueprints, ready to hire natives to help build the factory we have designed. Instead, we should be arriving with resources to motivate the natives to design their own factory and to help them figure out how to build and operate it themselves. Every bit of technical assistance that displaces a comparable capability on the part of the local society should be regarded as a two-edged sword and treated with great caution. Above all, the outsiders need to avoid the temptation to speed up the process by running the factory themselves.

What this implies in practice is that outsiders wanting to build administrative capacity, whether international financial institutions, bilateral donors, or nongovernmental organizations, will optimally need to make direct grants to government agencies in client countries to build capacity. They should not set precise conditions for how the resources are to be used but rather enforce strict accountability standards for certain kinds of results. This policy is meant to mimic the discipline that competitive markets impose on firms: Markets don't care whether the firm is organized as a partnership or a public joint stock company, whether it is centralized or decentralized, whether its first-tier divisions are geographical or functional, as long as it makes money. This is to a large measure the approach underlying the U.S. Millennium Challenge Account, which will provide grants in exchange for measurable performance. Under this concept, demand must exist already on the part of candidate recipients, and the manner in which they use the funds will not be subject to outside micromanagement as long as they produce measurable results.

This approach to capacity-building will work only if the donors are patient and do not care whether the factory produces goods in the short run. As I noted in Chapter 1, there is a conflict in donor goals between building institutional capacity and providing end-users with the services that the capacity is meant to produce. In the end, everyone wants the factory to run at full output, but it matters critically whether local people can operate the factory to meet local needs. It is hard to be optimistic about whether donors can ever be patient enough to focus on capacity-building at the expense of actual service provision, since their backers usually demand visible results.[6]

[6] There is, however, one small precedent that suggests such an approach might be possible. There is a quasigovernmental organization in Washington called the National Endowment for Democracy (NED) that was established in the 1970s to help promote democracy around the world. The NED has what is by Washington standards a miniscule annual budget of around $30 million (in fiscal year 2002), part of which it distributes directly and part of which it allocates to four allied organizations connected to the Democratic Party, the Republican Party, the U.S. Chamber of Commerce, and the AFL-CIO. (These organizations are the National Democratic Institute, the International Republican Institute, the, the Center for International Private Enterprise, and the Labor Solidarity Center, respectively) The NED's aid model is very different from that of its larger and much better endowed counterpart, the USAID. NED and its four U.S.-based grantees distribute money in tiny amounts ranging from a few thousand to a few hundred thousand dollars directly to a large variety of foreign political parties, nongovernmental organizations, women's organizations, labor unions, business organizations, and other civil society organizations that come to it seeking resources to accomplish some specific task. Neither NED nor its grantees actually run anything; administrative over-

The problem of the politicization of aid at bilateral agencies like the U.S. Agency for International Development (USAID) have been well understood for decades but don't seem to be readily fixable (Tendler 1975). The governments that will be recipients of aid do not control all of the variables leading to measurable improvements in performance. It may be possible to reform a telecommunications sector but not the state oil company, to fix fiscal policy but not public education. There may be real reform without it showing up in aggregate performance indicators. If some things work and others don't, the donors will have to resist the strong temptation to jump back into the micromanagement of reform.

It has been a longstanding dream of the social sciences to turn the study of human behavior into a true science, moving from mere description to formal models of causation with nontrivial predictive value, based on rigorous empirical observation. This project can be realized more readily in some spheres of human behavior than in others. Markets are susceptible to this kind of analysis, which is why economics emerged as the queen of the social sciences in the late twentieth century. But organizations constitute a complicated case. Individ-

---

head is taken up entirely in vetting the grantees and following up to hold them accountable for performing the tasks they set out to accomplish.

This delivery model differs sharply from that of USAID and other international aid agencies, which disburse money in much larger projects that often total hundreds of millions of dollars and which create large assistance infrastructures within the local countries. USAID is infamous for spending large sums of money on overhead and contractors—many of them U.S.-based—and seeing relatively little assistance going directly to groups in the client countries.

NED is by no means a perfect model for capacity-building; its mandate is too sweeping and its resources too small to contribute more than marginally to its core mission. Its focus is in any case on developing political parties and civil society rather than government agencies, but it suggests some general principles: Local groups are responsible for designing and implementing their projects from start to finish and receive resources directly without giving up control to the outside funder.

uals in organizations look out for their narrow self-interests, and to the extent they do, the economists's methodological individualism provides genuine insight. But to a much greater extent than in markets, norms and social ties affect individual choices in organizations. The effort to be more "scientific" than the underlying subject matter permits carries a real cost in blinding us to the real complexities of public administration as it is practiced in different societies.

3

WEAK STATES AND INTERNATIONAL
LEGITIMACY

In the first two chapters I discuss the problem of weak governance and missing or inadequate institutions at the nation-state level, where it becomes a critical obstacle to the economic development of individual poor countries. It has also become a critical problem at the level of the international system as a whole. Sovereignty and the nation-state, cornerstones of the Westphalian system, have been eroded in fact and attacked in principle because what goes on inside states—in other words, their internal governance—often matters intensely to other members of the international system. But who has the right or the legitimacy to violate another state's sovereignty, and for what purposes? Is there a source of international legitimacy that does not itself depend on the existence and strength of sovereign nation-states? If not, doesn't the attack on sovereignty become a self-contradictory enterprise? In this chapter, I address this set of interrelated problems.

Since the end of the Cold War, weak or failing states have arguably become the single most important problem for international order (Crocker 2003). Weak or failing states commit human rights abuses, provoke humanitarian disasters, drive massive waves of immigration, and attack their neighbors. Since September 11, it also has been clear that they shelter international terrorists who can do significant damage to the United States and other developed countries.

During the period from the fall of the Berlin Wall in 1989 to September 11, 2001, the vast majority of international crises centered around weak or failing states. These included Somalia, Haiti, Cambodia, Bosnia, Kosovo, Rwanda, Liberia, Sierra Leone, Congo, and East Timor. The international community in various guises stepped into each of these conflicts—often too late and with too few resources—and in several cases ended up literally taking over the governance function from local actors.

The September 11 attacks highlighted a different sort of problem. The failed state of Afghanistan was so weak that it could in effect be hijacked by a non-state actor, the terrorist organization al-Qaida, and serve as a base of global terrorist operations. The attacks drove home the ways in which violence had become democratized: The possibility of combining radical Islamism with weapons of mass destruction (WMD) suddenly meant that events going on in distant, chaotic parts of the globe could matter intensely to the United States and other rich and powerful countries. Traditional forms of deterrence or containment would not work against this type of non-state actor, so security concerns demanded reaching inside of states and changing their regime to prevent future threats from arising. The failed state problem that was seen previously as largely a humanitarian or human rights issue suddenly took on a major security dimension. In the words of Michael Ignatieff (2003), "It was also, in the 1990's, a general failure of the historical imagination, an inability of the post-cold-war West to grasp that the emerging crisis of state order in so many overlapping zones of the world—from Egypt to Afghanistan—would eventually become a security threat at home."

Apart from abjectly failed states like Somalia or Afghanistan, there was another type of governance problem driving international instability as well. Among the background causes of the turmoil in the Middle East is the lack of democracy, pluralism, or meaningful popular political participation in much of the Arab world (United Nations Development Program 2002). The increasingly authoritarian nature of rule in the region was seen as having been abetted by the United States, which was accused of having ulterior motives for its support of regimes like those in Saudi Arabia or Egypt. The area was, moreover, stagnant economically, having largely missed out on the waves of economic reform that characterized Latin America, Asia, and other parts of the developing world in the 1980s and 1990s. This stagnation (or regression as in Saudi Arabia, which saw its per capita gross domestic product fall by some two-thirds over a twenty-year period) came just at a point when these countries were experiencing a youth bulge and generating tens of thousands of unemployable young men. As in other parts of the developing world, much of this stagnation could be attributed to poor governance on the part of states that discouraged entrepreneurship and efficient markets. The Israeli-Palestinian conflict had its governance dimension as well: A major defect of the Oslo peace process in the 1990s was its failure to demand democratic accountability within the Palestinian authority or prevent high levels of corruption and rent-seeking there.

The New Empire

The logic of American foreign policy since September 11 is driving it toward a situation in which it either takes on responsibility for the governance of weak states or else it throws the problem in the lap of the international community. While denying that it has imperial ambitions, the Bush administration has nonetheless articulated, in the president's June 2002 West Point speech and in the *National Security Strategy of the United States* (2002), a doctrine of preemption or, more properly, preventive war that in effect will put the United States in a position of governing potentially hostile populations in countries that threaten it with terrorism. This happened in Afghanistan in 2001. The Karzai government, far more decent and forward looking than the Taliban regime it replaced, was put in place by the United States and survives largely with the support of American power. Its power is contested by various warlords around the country and its legitimacy questioned by surviving pockets of Taliban fighters. The need to fight the war in Afghanistan drew American military power into countries like Tajikistan, Turkmenistan, and Uzbekistan, all of which were formerly within the Soviet sphere of influence and all of which have severe problems of internal governance.

In March 2003, the United States took on the even more ambitious project of toppling the Baathist regime in Iraq and transforming the country into a functioning democracy. In a speech given on February 26, 2003, President Bush stated: "We meet here during a crucial period in the history of our nation, and of the civilized world. Part of that history was written by others; the rest will be written by us." He laid out an extraordinary agenda that involved not just the democratization of Iraq but also the transformation of the politics of much of the Middle East, including progress on the Israeli-Palestinian dispute and the promotion of pluralism in other parts of the Arab world.

Iraq aside, the terrorist attacks that took place in Mombasa, Kenya, Bali, Indonesia, and Riyadh, Saudi Arabia in 2002 and 2003 highlighted the fact that al-Qaida continues to take advantage of opportunities provided by poorly governed states. The United States is clearly not going to intervene directly with its own forces in every state around the world where terrorists operate and must therefore rely on the ability of local states to control terrorism themselves. Their frequent inability to do so highlights the kinds of gaps in institutional capability discussed in Chapters 1 and 2. Neither the Kenyan nor Indonesian governments were able to act decisively to forestall the attacks, and while the Indonesian regime made relatively good progress prosecuting the perpetrators, it could act only with substantial foreign assistance. The United States in its pursuit of security thus arrives back at precisely the kinds of questions faced by international development agencies of how to externally stimulate state-building in countries with severe internal dysfunction.

The Erosion of Sovereignty

Weak governance undermines the principle of sovereignty on which the post-Westphalian international order has been built. It does so because the problems that weak states generate for themselves and for others vastly increase the likelihood that someone else in the international system will seek to intervene in their affairs against their wishes to forcibly fix the problem. *Weak* here refers to state strength and not scope, to use the terminology developed earlier, meaning a lack of institutional capacity to implement and enforce policies, often driven by an underlying lack of legitimacy of the political system as a whole.

Many people critical of the Bush administration's new doctrine of preemption and war with Iraq see it as a radical shift from earlier policies that emphasized deterrence and containment, precisely because it depends on the periodic violation of sovereignty (Hassner 2002). In fact, the grounds for the erosion of sovereignty were laid much earlier in the so-called humanitarian interventions of the 1990s. The experience of Somalia, Haiti, Cambodia, the Balkans, and other places has generated a huge literature on external intervention (see, among others,

Damrosch 1993; Heiberg 1994; Hoffmann 1996; Lugo 1996; Mastanduno and Lyons 1995; Mayall 1996; Murphy 1996; von Lipsey 1997; Weiss and Collins 1996; and Williamson 1998; for a critical view, see Carpenter 1997).

In the debates over humanitarian intervention, the case was made that the Westphalian system was no longer an adequate framework for international relations. The Westphalian system was built around a deliberate agnosticism over the question of legitimacy. The end of the Cold War, it was argued, brought about much greater consensus within the world community over the principles of political legitimacy and human rights than before. Sovereignty and therefore legitimacy could no longer be automatically conferred on the de facto power holder in a country. State sovereignty was a fiction or bad joke in the case of countries like Somalia or Afghanistan, which had descended into rule by warlords. Dictators and human rights abusers like Serbia's Milosevic could not hide behind the principle of sovereignty to protect themselves as they committed crimes against humanity, particularly in multiethnic states like the former Yugoslavia where the borders of the sovereign state in question were themselves contested. Under these circumstances, outside powers, acting in the name of human rights and democratic legitimacy, had not just the right but the obligation to intervene.

The humanitarian interventions of the 1990s led to an extension of a de facto international imperial power over the "failed state" part of the world. The interventions were often spearheaded by American military power but followed up on the nation-building side by a large coalition of primarily European countries, Australia, New Zealand, and Japan. In Somalia, Cambodia, Bosnia, Kosovo, East Timor, and now Afghanistan, the "international community" ceased to be an abstraction and took on a palpable presence as the effective government of the country in question. In these countries, sovereignty had ceased to exist, and governance functions were displaced to the

United Nations or other aid agencies and nongovernmental organizations (NGOs)—in the case of East Timor, located on a ship floating in the harbor outside of the capital of Dili. This international imperium may be a well-meaning one based on human rights and democracy, but it was an imperium nonetheless and set a precedent for the surrender of sovereignty to governance by international agencies.

The problem that faces the United States is that failed governance can create intolerable security threats in the form of terrorists wielding WMD. Some people like to draw a sharp distinction between interventions for the sake of promoting human rights within a country and interventions to prevent security threats to other countries, and say that only the former are legitimate grounds for the violation of sovereignty. This distinction is questionable because it presumes that self-defense is somehow less legitimate than the defense of others. In any case, these issues often overlap in practice because the governments that commit human rights violations often also threaten their neighbors or are too weak to prevent such threats and abuses from arising.

This point should not be interpreted as making a brief for the Bush administration's war with Iraq. The pros and cons of that case were very complex. The possibilities for deterring a genuine security threat from Baghdad were not adequately explored, and the administration conflated the threat posed by Iraq with the terrorist threat in ways that did not accurately reflect the differing interests of the two parties (Mearsheimer 2002). The point is rather that the existence of WMD in the hands of non-state actors poses a new and extremely severe type of security problem that would almost certainly justify intervention on the part of a country threatened in that manner. Deterrence does not operate where the likelihood of the first use of WMD is substantial. The principle of sovereignty by itself would never be sufficient to protect a country that was sheltering this kind of threat. Fixing this problem then leads to exactly the same result as humanitarian intervention: the need to go into such countries and take over their governance to eliminate such threats and prevent them from arising again in the future.

Nation-Building

The kinds of issues raised in the first two chapters—how to promote governance of weak states, improve their democratic legitimacy, and strengthen self-sustaining institutions—thus becomes the central project of contemporary international politics. We arrive at this conclusion either as a result of our desire to reconstruct conflict-ridden or war-torn societies, out of a desire to eliminate spawning grounds for terrorism, or out of a hope that poor countries will have a chance to develop economically. If there is a science, art, or *techné* to state-building, then it will serve all of these goals simultaneously and be in extremely high demand.

In the United States, this effort has come to be known as nation-building. This terminology perhaps reflects the national experience, in which cultural and historical identity was heavily shaped by political institutions like constitutionalism and democracy. Europeans tend to be more aware of the distinction between state and nation and point out that nation-building in the sense of the creation of a community bound together by shared history and culture is well beyond the ability of any outside power to achieve. They are, of course, right; only states can be deliberately constructed. If a nation arises from this, it is more a matter of luck than design.

In the United States, there has been an ideologized debate over nation-building. Some conservatives, including many on the libertarian right, are opposed in principle to nation-building because they do not think it is feasible and do not like the idea of open-ended and expensive commitments to what they regard as a kind of international welfare. On the other side, there are many in the international financial institution (IFI), donor, and NGO communities who talk about nation-building as if it were a process we understand well and could accomplish if only we had the resources. The first position is simply untenable given the kinds of security and foreign policy needs the United States faces and will face. The Bush administration came into office skeptical about nation-building but has willy-nilly gotten dragged into it in Afghanistan and Iraq. Those who favor nation-building have to face squarely an extremely troubled record of success in this area. It is not simply that nation-building hasn't worked; in cases like sub-Saharan Africa, many of these efforts have actually eroded institutional capacity over time. We need therefore to take a hard look at what is and is not possible and understand where the limits on what outside aid can accomplish lie.

There are three distinct aspects or phases to nation-building. The first concerns what has come to be called post-conflict reconstruction and applies to countries emerging from violent conflict like Afghanistan, Somalia, and Kosovo, where state authority has collapsed completely and needs to be rebuilt from the ground up. Here the issue for outside powers is the short-term provision of stability through infusions of security forces, police, humanitarian relief, and technical assistance to restore electricity, water, banking and payment systems, and so on.

If the collapsed state is lucky enough to achieve a modicum of stability with international help (as in the case of Bosnia), the second phase comes into play. Here the chief objective is to create self-sustaining state institutions that can survive the withdrawal of outside intervention. This phase is much more difficult to achieve than the first but is critical if outside powers are ever to make a graceful exit from the country in question.

The third aspect overlaps with the second to a considerable

degree. It has to do with the strengthening of weak states, where state authority exists in a reasonably stable form but cannot accomplish certain necessary state functions like the protection of property rights or the provision of basic primary education. This category is very broad and extends from states that have pockets of institutional expertise in areas like central banking and exchange rate management but have trouble delivering low-specificity services like education or rule of law (e.g., Peru, Mexico) to countries where institutions are weak across the board (e.g., Kenya, Ghana).

Afghanistan and post-Saddam Iraq pose very different challenges. Afghanistan never had a modern state. Under the monarchy that existed up to the beginning of its political troubles in the 1970s, it largely remained a tribal confederation with minimal state penetration outside of the capital Kabul. The subsequent years of communist misrule and civil war eliminated everything that was left of that already weak state. State-building after the ouster of the Taliban had to begin from the ground up, with resources and guidance provided entirely from the outside. Given the magnitude of the task and the relative stinginess of the United States and other donors, the prospects for putting a modern state in place (much less a democracy) look daunting.

Iraq, by contrast, was a more highly developed country with much greater resources, both material and human. Here the problem was that functioning state institutions either collapsed or were dismantled by the United States in the immediate aftermath of the war and needed to be rebuilt. A huge amount of administrative capacity was lost to the widespread looting and disorder that followed the intervention. As in the case of postwar Germany and Japan and many post-communist regimes, state-building in post-Saddam Iraq was hobbled by the need to prevent the re-emergence of members of the old regime. A generation of totalitarian rule has clear-cut the political landscape and left few people outside the ruling party and military with administrative competence or political skill.

The United States and the international community have had a mixed record in dealing with failed states in the first phase of post-conflict reconstruction or stabilization. The United States and other international players made plenty of mistakes in Panama, Somalia, Haiti, and Bosnia in organizing these activities, but a certain amount of learning occurred as well. By the time of the Kosovo and East Timor nation-building initiatives in 1999 and 2000, both the U.S. government and the international community had devised much better means of internal coordination and some mechanisms for preserving institutional memory about nation-building.

Unfortunately, the Bush administration failed to draw on this prior experience when it entered Afghanistan and Iraq, and committed many of the same mistakes that were made in previous nation-building exercises (e.g., not anticipating widespread looting and failing to provide police or constabulary forces to deal with civil disorder). In Iraq this was due in part to the unilateral way in which the administration went into the war, which left it mostly bereft of international partners for its effort, and in part to internal bureaucratic struggles that left organization of the reconstruction effort in the hands of the Pentagon (Fukuyama 2004). The U.S. Department of Defense, while a critical player in any nation-building exercise, lacked the institutional capability to organize such a complex operation. Hence, state-building is something needed not just in collapsed or weak Third World states but occasionally in Washington as well (Mendelson Forman 2002).

If the international community has had some limited success in dealing with immediate post-conflict reconstruction, its record is much less impressive in dealing with the second stage of nation-building, wherein outside actors seek to establish or strengthen legitimate, self-sustaining political institutions that eventually allow the government in question to wean itself from outside assistance.

Here the imperial experience of the 1990s in Somalia, Haiti, Cambodia, Bosnia, Kosovo, and East Timor should be very chastening. Neither the United State nor the international community has made much headway in creating self-sustaining states in any of the countries it has set out to rebuild. These nation-building exercises have played a critical role in stabilizing the situation on the ground and paving the way for negotiated settlements. Peace is of inestimable benefit to the people living in those countries and justifies the international effort. But the rhetoric of the international community stresses "capacity-building" while the reality has been rather a kind of "capacity sucking out," to use Ignatieff's (2002) memorable phrase. The international community, including the vast numbers of NGOs that are an intimate part of it, comes so richly endowed and full of capabilities that it tends to crowd out rather than complement the extremely weak state capacities of the targeted countries. This means that while governance functions are performed, indigenous capacity does not increase, and the countries in question are likely to revert to their former situations once the international community loses interest or moves on to the next crisis area.

Bosnia is a revealing case. Seven years after the conclusion of the Dayton Accord that brought the Bosnian war to an end, the country continued to be governed by the United Nations Office of the High Representative in Bosnia and Herzegovina (OHR). There was no meaningful democracy in Bosnia, despite the holding of elections; the OHR used its powers to dismiss presidents, prime ministers, judges, mayors, and other elected officials. It could pass legislation and create new institutions without reference to the preferences of the Bosnian people. Much of the administrative capacity of the Bosnian government lay in the hands of international experts rather than indigenous civil servants, to the point that some observers compared it to the British Raj (Knaus and Martin 2003). Despite the international community's heavy investments in Kosovo—or perhaps because of them—something similar took place there.

None of this should be taken to imply that these outside interventions were not worthwhile, since they came in response to humanitarian crises or severe postconflict situations. Solving the short-term problem and kicking the long-term institutional can down the road is often all one can do in such circumstances. The success of nation-building is thus usually measured by a less demanding metric, such as recovery of GDP to preconflict levels or the holding of a democratic election (Dobbins et al. 2003).

It is not clear, given the low to nonexistent level of stateness in many failed states, whether there is any real alternative to a quasi-permanent, quasi-colonial relationship between the "beneficiary" country and the international community. In a sense, the latter has recreated the earlier mandatory system of the League of Nations period in which certain colonial powers were given explicit charter to govern a given territory on its behalf. The problem with our current system is that contemporary norms do not accept the legitimacy of anything other than self-government, which makes us then insist that whatever governance we do provide be temporary and rule transitional. Since we do not in fact know how to transfer institutional capacity in a hurry, we are setting ourselves and our supposed beneficiaries up for large disappointments.

Democratic Legitimacy at an International Level

The big arguments are not over the principle of sovereignty per se, which few people are willing to defend in a pure form any longer. It is clear that not all sovereignties are created equal and that poor governance contributes directly to downgrading of the international community's respect for a country's sovereignty. This shift, to repeat, did not occur after September 11 but rather was developed in the course of the humanitarian interventions of the 1990s.

The argument among members of the international community today focuses instead on the question of who gets to decide on whose sovereignty to violate, and on what grounds. To what extent does it remain the prerogative of sovereign nation-states, and to what degree must such decisions be constrained by international laws or norms? These questions take us into the domain of a different set of democratic legitimacy issues, this time focused not so much on individual states but on the international system. This debate has exposed an enormous gulf between the United States and its European allies, which is likely to be a neuralgic source of friction for some time to come.

While Europeans were initially quite supportive of the United States in the aftermath of the September 11 attacks, there was a large upsurge of criticism and, in many cases, outright anti-Americanism in the period after the end of the war in Afghanistan in late 2001. Much of this centered on European charges of American unilateralism on issues like the treatment of al-Qaida prisoners in Guantánamo Bay, the American abrogation of the antiballistic missile treaty, Washington's failure to join the International Criminal Court, and, earlier, the Bush administration's announcement that it was withdrawing from the Kyoto Protocol on global warming. The most serious rift, however, emerged over Washington's intention to attack Iraq in order to effect "regime change" and eliminate its WMD. This led to one of the most serious rifts in European-American relations since the Suez Crisis of 1956, with German Chancellor Gerhard Schröder running for and winning reelection on a platform overtly opposed to U.S. foreign policy and France and Germany organizing active opposition to a second United Nations resolution authorizing the war.

The European opponents of American unilateralism have argued that they have been trying to construct a genuine rule-based international order suitable to the circumstances of the post–Cold War world. That world, free of sharp ideological conflicts and large-scale military competition, is one that gives substantially more room for consensus, dialogue, and negotiation as ways of settling disputes. They are horrified by the Bush administration's announcement of a virtually open-ended doctrine of preemption against terrorists or states that sponsor terrorists, in which the United States alone decides when and where to use force.

The view that Americans are unilateralist and Europeans are committed to a broad, multilateral world order is of course a great oversimplification. Liberal internationalism, after all, has a long and honored place in American foreign policy. The United States was the country that promoted the League of Nations, the United Nations, the Bretton Woods institutions, the General Agreement on Tariffs and Trade, the World Trade Organization (WTO), and a host of other international organizations. There are many international governance organizations in the world today in which the United States participates as an active, if not the most active, member, addressing issues from standards setting, nuclear power safety, and scientific cooperation to aviation safety, bank settlements, drug regulation, uses of outer space, and telecommunications.

In the realm of economics, the United States has expended a great deal of effort over the past generation trying to promote a liberal multilateral trade and investment regime with increasingly autonomous dispute-resolution capabilities. The motives for this effort are obvious: Americans benefit strongly from and indeed dominate the global economy, which is why globalization bears a "made in the USA" label. In this realm, the Europeans don't have a particularly good record with regard to multilateralism. There are a number of areas where the Europeans have acted unilaterally in economic matters and in ways that at times contravene the existing legal order. The EU resisted unfavorable decisions against it on bananas for nine years, and beef hormones for even longer. It has announced a precautionary principle with regard to genetically modified foods, which is very difficult to reconcile with the WTO's sanitary and phytosanitary rules. Indeed, the Europeans have been violating their own rules with regard to genetically modified foods, with certain member states setting standards different from those of the union itself. The European Competition Commission under Mario Monti successfully blocked the merger of U.S. firms General Electric and Honeywell when the deal had been approved by American and Canadian regulators, in ways that promoted suspicions that the EU was simply acting to protect specific European interests. Finally, the EU has succeeded in exporting its data privacy rules to the United States through its safe harbor arrangements.

It is thus hard to argue that the Europeans have a substantially better record with regard to multilateralism than the United States in economic matters. Both have violated international rules when it has been convenient, while asserting the importance of a rule-based international order. The worst area is agriculture, where U.S. and European subsidies to domestic producers impose enormous costs on poor countries. The welfare costs of the EU's Common Agricultural Policy have been well understood for many years and amount to hundreds of millions of dollars of lost revenues for countries in Africa, the Middle East, and elsewhere. While pushing for a Doha Round of trade talks that would deal with agriculture, the United States in 2002 passed an agriculture bill that sharply increased subsidies and protections for domestic U.S. producers. The African country of Mali, for example, receives some $37 million annually in grants from the U.S. Agency for International Development but will lose some $43 million in cotton revenues as a result of new subsidies in the bill (Edmund L. Andrews, "Rich Nations are Criticized for Enforcing Trade Barriers," *New York Times*, Sept. 30 2002).

The most serious disputes over unilateralism lie in the area of security and have dominated the agenda since September 11. After hinting that it might not need to go to the United Nations to seek authorization for military action against Iraq, the United States did in fact seek Security Council support in September 2002 and in the course of the fall procured a unanimous vote for U.N. Security Council Resolution 1441, renewing demands for Iraqi compliance to earlier resolutions mandating the dismantling and destruction of its WMD stocks. The United States was on relatively strong ground with regard to the finding that Iraq stood in violation of international law—both a series of earlier disarmament resolutions and Resolution 1441. But the Bush administration also made clear that it would not take no for an answer from the Security Council and would proceed with military action against Iraq regardless of the views of the veto-bearing permanent members.

The issue at stake here is an important one from the standpoint of rules regarding sovereignty and security. Article 51 of the United Nations Charter permits members to undertake military actions unilaterally in their own self-defense, which could easily be construed to include cases of preemption where a country faces imminent military attack. Iraq did not fall under this rubric, and the Bush administration didn't try to justify its actions under an Article 51 exemption. Iraq did not pose an immediate threat to the United States; military action against it fell more in the category of preventive rather than preemptive war. The United States argued with considerable justice that WMD, and nuclear weapons in particular, pose a special problem because they represent a genie that is hard to put back in the bottle. On the other hand, the right of states to launch preventive wars in anticipation of such threats cannot be a good general principle of international relations. The United States would surely object if Russia or China asserted such a general right; what it is asking, in effect, is that the world community delegate to it alone the discretion to act in this fashion.

It is possible to argue that these differences between the United States and Europe are the product of a rather maladroit handling of allies by this particular administration. A great deal of European irritation with the United States arises from stylistic matters and from the Bush administration's strange failure to consult, explain, justify, and cajole in the manner of previous administrations. The administration could have let ratification of Kyoto languish in Congress as the Clinton administration did, rather than casually announcing withdrawal from the pact at a luncheon for NATO ambassadors. Europeans did not like the religious language of the "axis of evil" phrase used in President Bush's January 2002 State of the Union address, nor the fact that this major policy shift was announced on the fly without prior notification or explanation. The United States has had a consistent record of using strong-arm tactics to shape international agreements to its liking, and then to walk away from them at the last moment. This pattern goes all the way back to Woodrow Wilson and the League of Nations and was continued in negotiations over the Rio Pact, Kyoto, and the ICC.

Underlying the current disputes is a much more fundamental difference in principle between the United States and many European countries over the source of democratic legitimacy on an international level. To put it rather schematically and oversimply, Americans tend not to see any source of democratic legitimacy higher than the constitutional democratic nation-state. To the extent that any international organization like the United Nations has legitimacy, it is because duly constituted democratic majorities have handed that legitimacy up to them in a negotiated, intergovernmental process. Such legitimacy can be withdrawn at any time by the contracting parties; international law and organization has no existence independent of this type of voluntary agreement between sovereign nation-states.

Europeans, by contrast, tend to believe that democratic legitimacy flows from the will of an international community much larger than any individual nation-state. This international community is not embodied concretely in a single, global democratic constitutional order, yet it hands down legitimacy to existing international institutions, which are seen as partially embodying it. Thus, peacekeeping forces in the former Yugoslavia are not merely ad hoc intergovernmental arrangements but rather moral expressions of the will and norms of the larger international community.

The European view of international legitimacy in many ways parallels the European view of legitimacy on a nation-state level. As Nettl (1968) and Huntington (1981) have pointed out, many countries, particularly in continental Europe, have always had a concept of the state as the guardian of the public interest standing above the particular interests of the state's citizens. This state, usually embodied in a professional permanent bureaucracy, at times has to lean against the popular will because it has a clearer view of the common interest of the nation. The Lockean liberal view of the state that prevails in the United States, by contrast, sees no public interest apart from the aggregated interests of the individuals who make up a society. The state is the servant of the people and has no views of the common interest apart from what is democratically ratified by them. As I noted in Chapter 2, democratic publics can delegate executive authority to the state for certain critical decisions, but the state retains no fundamental autonomy.

When these ideas are applied at an international level, it is easy to see how Europeans have come to view a variety of international organizations as custodians of a common global good that stands above and apart from the wishes of individual nation-states. Just as the state on a national level retains considerable autonomy in making decisions for the public good, so too do Europeans tend to accord international bodies more authority in determining global common interests. For the United States, by contrast, the delegation of authority on

both a national and international level is much more circumscribed. If a given international institution does not serve the
interests of a democratically constituted nation-state, the latter has the right to limit or take back its participation in it
(Rabkin 1998).

There are multiple reasons why this difference on international legitimacy exists between the United States and Europe.
Robert Kagan (2003) has argued that it is based on the relative
power of the United States over Europe. The Europeans, he argues, like international law and norms because they are much
weaker than the United States, and the latter likes unilateralism because it is significantly more powerful than any other
country or group of countries (like the EU) not just in terms of
military power but also economically, technologically, and
culturally.

It is of course undeniable that small, weak countries that are
acted on rather than influencing others naturally prefer to live
in a world of norms, laws, and institutions, in which more
powerful nations are constrained. Conversely, a "sole super-
power" like the United States would obviously like to see its
freedom of action be as unencumbered as possible.

But to point to differences in power is to beg the question of
why these differentials exist. The EU collectively encompasses
a population of 375 million people and has a GDP of $9.7 tril-
lion, compared to a U.S. population of 280 million and a GDP
of $10.1 trillion. Europe could certainly spend money on de-
fense at a level that would put it on a par with the United
States, but it chooses not to. Europe spends barely $130 billion
collectively on defense—a sum that has been steadily falling—
compared to U.S. defense spending of $300 billion, which is
due to rise sharply. Despite Europe's turn in a more conservative direction in 2002, not one rightist or center-right candidate is campaigning on a platform of significantly raising defense spending. Europe's ability to deploy its power is of course
greatly weakened by the collective action problems posed by

the current system of EU decision making, but the failure to create more useable military power is clearly a political and normative issue.

The reasons for this normative difference lie, of course, at the very heart of the postwar European project. The states of Western Europe concluded at the end of the World War II that it was precisely the unbridled exercise of national sovereignty that got them into trouble through two world wars in the twentieth century (Ikenberry and Hall 1989). The house that they have been building for themselves since the 1950s called the European Union was deliberately intended to embed those sovereignties in multiple layers of rules, norms, and regulations to prevent those sovereignties from ever spinning out of control again. Kupchan (2002) argues that the EU is a mechanism for aggregating and projecting power beyond Europe's borders. This view is almost certainly wrong: Most Europeans see the EU's purpose as one of transcending power politics altogether. Thus the continent that invented the very idea of the modern state built around centralized power and the ability to deploy military force has eliminated the very core of stateness from its identity. This was the case above all in Germany where, as Peter Katzenstein (1997) has shown, postwar identity was constructed around a kind of antisovereignty project. German freedom of action would henceforth be constrained by multiple layers of international constraints, above all the EU but including other international organizations up through and including the United Nations. Germans for many years after World War II taught their children not to display the German flag or cheer too loudly for German teams at football matches. The kind of patriotism Americans displayed in the aftermath of September 11 is thus quite foreign and, indeed, distasteful to them—and would, if displayed by the Germans themselves, be distasteful to everyone else.

The American view of stateness and sovereignty is very different. Seymour Martin Lipset has explained in a series of books how the United States is an outlier among developed democracies, with policies and institutions that differ significantly from those of Europe, Canada, Australia, New Zealand, and Japan (Lipset 1981, 1990, 1995). Whether in regard to welfare, crime, regulation, education, or foreign policy, there are constant differences separating America from everyone else: It is consistently more antistatist, individualistic, laissez-faire, and egalitarian than other democracies. This sense of exceptionalism extends to its own democratic institutions and their legitimacy. Unlike most of the old societies of Europe, the United States was founded on the basis of a political idea. There was no American people or nation prior to the founding of the country: National identity is civic rather than religious, cultural, racial, or ethnic. There has been only one American regime, which, as the world's oldest continuously existing democracy, is not viewed as a transient political compromise. This means that the country's political institutions have always been imbued with an almost religious reverence that Europeans, with more ancient sources of identity, find peculiar.

Moreover, for Americans, their Declaration of Independence and Constitution are not just the basis of a legal-political order on the North American continent; they are the embodiment of universal values and have a significance for humankind that goes well beyond the borders of the United States. When President Reagan repeatedly quoted Governor Winthrop in speaking of the United States as a "shining city on a hill," his words had great resonance for many Americans. This feeling leads at times to a typically American tendency to confuse its own national interests with the broader interests of the world as a whole.

The situation of Europe—as well as developed Asian societies like Japan, for that matter—is very different. Europeans and the Japanese were peoples with shared histories long before they were democracies. They have other sources of identity besides politics. They have seen a variety of regimes come and go, and some of those regimes have, in living memory, been responsible for very shameful acts. While the French and, in a different way, the British continue to feel a sense of broader national mission in the world, it is safe to say that few other European countries regard their own political institutions as universal models for the rest of the world to follow. Indeed, many Europeans regard their national institutions as having a much lower degree of legitimacy than international ones, with the EU occupying a place somewhere in between.

Beyond the Nation-State

Americans and Europeans have different views about the source of legitimacy at an international level, with Americans believing it is rooted in the will of democratic majorities in constitutional nation-states and Europeans tending to believe it is based on principles of justice higher than the laws or wills of particular nation states. Both sides come to their views for reasons deeply rooted in their own national histories and in that sense are quite understandable.

The European view is correct in an abstract sense but wrong in practice. Many Europeans assert that they and not the Americans are the true advocates of universal liberal values because they believe in such values independently of their embodiment in actual democratic nation-states. Decisions by sovereign liberal democracies that are correct procedurally are not guaranteed to be just or in accordance with these higher principles. Democratic majorities can decide to do terrible things to other countries and can violate human rights and norms of decency on which their own democratic order is based. Indeed, the Lincoln-Douglas debates were over this precise issue. Douglas argued that he cared not whether the people voted slavery up or down, as long as the decision reflected the will of the people. Lincoln by contrast said that slavery in itself violated the higher principle of human equality on which the American regime was based. The legitimacy of the actions of a democracy are not in the end based on democratic procedural correctness but on the prior rights and norms that come from a moral realm higher than that of the legal order.

The problem with the European position is that while such a higher realm of liberal democratic values might theoretically exist, it is very imperfectly embodied in any given international institution. The very idea that this legitimacy is handed downward from a disembodied international level rather than handed upward from concrete, legitimate democratic publics on a nation-state level virtually invites abuse on the part of elites who are then free to interpret the will of the international community to suit their own preferences.

The second important practical problem with the European position is that of enforcement. The one power that is unique to sovereign nation-states, even in today's globalized world, is the power to enforce laws. Even if existing international laws and organizations did accurately reflect the will of the international community (whatever that means), enforcement remains by and large the province of nation-states. A great deal of both international and national law coming out of Europe consists of what amounts to social policy wish lists that are completely unenforceable. Europeans justify these kinds of laws by saying they are expressions of social objectives; Americans reply, correctly in my view, that such unenforceable aspirations undermine the rule of law itself.

The same problem of enforcement exists on the international level. The "international community" is a fiction insofar as any enforcement capability depends entirely on the action of individual nation-states. There is no autonomous United Nations or, indeed, European military. All international organizations dealing with serious pending security matters (as opposed to postconflict peacekeeping missions) face crippling collective action problems. During the Cold War these were sufficient to prevent the UN Security Council from taking any meaningful enforcement actions, with the exception of the Korean War, when the mistaken Soviet boycott allowed authorization of UN intervention. Even for organizations less ideologically diverse than the UN like the EU and NATO, decisive collective action has been extremely difficult to achieve. The only exceptions to this during the 1990s were the first Gulf War and Kosovo, neither of which could have come about without the United States taking a large leadership position and strong-arming reluctant allies.

The history of the Balkans in the 1990s illustrates the weaknesses of the European view of international action. All of the countries of the EU agreed that Serbia under Milosevic was the source of both grave human rights abuses in both Bosnia and Kosovo, that the conflict was highly destabilizing for Europe, and that it should be a largely European responsibility to bring order and justice to the region. The Europeans did in fact intervene by imposing an embargo on the region (one that benefited the Serbs more than the Bosnians) and by sending peacekeepers into the region. What they were unable to do, however, was to collectively decide to deploy a decisive degree of military power to unseat Milosevic, democratize Serbia, and thereby get to the root of the problem. In fact, the European peacekeepers contributed to the problem by not being willing to fight; in places like Srebrenica, they were held hostage and needed to be rescued. It was only as a result of actions by states that were willing to decisively use traditional forms of military power— the Croatians in the case of Bosnia and the Americans in the case of Kosovo—that Serbian domination was ended and the Balkans pacified.

Robert Kagan put the matter in the following manner. The Europeans are the ones who actually believe they are living at the end of history–that is, in a largely peaceful world that to an increasing degree can be governed by law, norms, and international agreements. In this world, power politics and classical realpolitik have become obsolete. Americans, by contrast, think they are still living in history, and need to use traditional power-political means to deal with threats from Iraq, al-Qaida, North Korea, and other malignant forces. According to Kagan, the Europeans are half right: They have indeed created an end-of-history world for themselves within the EU, where sovereignty has given way to supranational organization. What they don't understand, however, is that the peace and safety of their European bubble is guaranteed ultimately by American military power.

Stateness has been eroded from another quarter as well. A variety of multilateral and international organizations have emerged that have been designed to take over certain governance functions from nation-states. Their ability to do this effectively varies enormously. Some, like the bewildering variety of standards-setting and technical organizations, actually do create international rules that are obeyed and greatly improve global efficiency. Others that are more political in nature have tended to erode the legitimacy of nation-states without putting effective international institutions in their place. Whether the United States took a correct approach to Iraq remains an open question, but we should not let the specific circumstances of this case divert attention from the fact that there is a potentially serious mismatch between the demand for security in a world of weak or failed states and the ability of international institutions to supply it.

Much of the argument over Iraq revolves around the empirical question of whether the world is as dangerous as the Bush administration says it is or whether the threats posed by countries like Iraq and North Korea can be better dealt with in other ways. (It is an empirical question in the sense that a factual answer exists; it may not be knowable, however, based on the information available to us now.) No one could argue that if a state built nuclear weapons and was determined to give them to terrorists to detonate on another state's territory, that latter state should not have to rely on international institutions to defend itself. On the other hand, if this threat is gravely exaggerated, then the preventive American response could in itself become the chief source of global instability.

4

SMALLER BUT STRONGER

For well over a generation, the trend in world politics has been to weaken stateness. This trend came about for both normative and economic reasons. Many states in the twentieth century were too powerful: They tyrannized populations and committed aggression against neighbors. Those that were not dictatorships nonetheless impeded economic growth and accumulated a variety of dysfunctions and inefficiencies due to excessive state scope. The trend therefore has been to cut back the size of state sectors and to turn over to the market or to civil society functions that have been improperly appropriated. At the same time, the growth of the global economy has tended to erode the autonomy of sovereign nation-states by increasing the mobility of information, capital, and, to a lesser extent, labor.

These changes were, by and large, all to the good. The agenda of reducing the scope of nation-states still remains a live one in many parts of the world: The stagnation that emerged in Japan during the 1990s and the social security crisis that will emerge in many European welfare states in the twenty-first century is linked to an excessive degree of regulation and state intervention in the economies of these countries.

For the post–September 11 period, the chief issue for global politics will not be how to cut back on stateness but how to build it up. For individual societies and for the global community, the withering away of the state is not a prelude to utopia but to disaster. A critical issue facing poor countries that blocks their possibilities for economic development is their inadequate level of institutional development. They do not need extensive states, but they do need strong and effective ones within the limited scope of necessary state functions.

In the international system, stateness has been under attack and eroded de facto for a variety of reasons. States throughout the less-developed world are weak, and the end of the Cold War led to the emergence of a band of failed and troubled states from Europe to South Asia. These weak states have posed threats to international order because they are the source of conflict and grave abuses of human rights and because they have become potential breeding grounds for a new kind of terrorism that can reach into the developed world. Strengthening these states through various forms of nation-building is a task that has become vital to international security but is one that few developed countries have mastered. Learning to do state-building better is thus central to the future of world order.

While we do not want to return to a world of clashing great powers, we do need to be mindful of the need for power. What only states and states alone are able to do is aggregate and purposefully deploy legitimate power. This power is necessary to enforce a rule of law domestically, and it is necessary to preserve world order internationally. Those who have argued for a "twilight of sovereignty"—whether they are proponents of free markets on the right or committed multilateralists on the left—have to explain what will replace the power of sovereign nation-states in the contemporary world (see Evans 1997). What has de facto filled that gap is a motley collection of multinational corporations, nongovernmental organizations, international organizations, crime syndicates, terrorist groups, and so forth that may have some degree of power or some degree of legitimacy but seldom both at the same time. In the absence of a clear answer, we have no choice but to turn back to the sovereign nation-state and to try to understand once again how to make it strong and effective.

On the other hand, the kind of traditional military power we associate with nation-states is clearly not sufficient to meet their needs. The Europeans are right that there are forms of soft power, like nation-building, that count. Countries have to be able to construct state institutions not just within their own borders but in other more disorganized and dangerous countries as well. In years past, they would have done this simply by invading the country and adding it administratively to their empire. Now we insist that we are promoting democracy, self-government, and human rights, and that any effort to rule other people is merely transitional rather than imperial in ambition. Whether the Europeans know significantly more than Americans about how to square this circle remains to be seen. In any event, the art of state-building will be a key component of national power, as important as the ability to deploy traditional military force to the maintenance of world order.

BIBLIOGRAPHY

Akerlof, George A. 1982. "Labor Contracts as Partial Gift Exchange," *Quarterly Journal of Economics* 47(4): 543–69.
——. 1970. "The Market for 'Lemons': Quality Uncertainty and the Market Mechanism," *Quarterly Journal of Economics* 84: 488–500.
Alchian, Armen A. 1950. "Uncertainty, Evolution, and Economic Theory," *Journal of Political Economy* 58: 211–21.
Alchian, Armen A., and Demsetz, H. 1972. "Production, Information Costs, and Economic Organization," *American Economic Review* 62(5): 777–95.
Allison, Graham T. Jr. 1971. *Essence of Decision* (Boston: Little, Brown).
Amsden, Alice H. 1989. *Asia's Next Giant: South Korea and Late Industrialization* (New York: Oxford University Press).
Barnard, Chester. 1938. *The Functions of the Executive* (Cambridge, MA: Harvard University Press).
Barro, Robert J. 1997. *Determinants of Economic Growth: A Cross-Country Survey* (Cambridge, MA: MIT Press).
Bates, Robert. 1983. *Essays on the Political Economy of Rural Africa* (Berkeley, CA: University of California Press).
——. 1981. *Markets and States in Tropical Africa: The Political Basis of Agricultural Policies* (Berkeley, CA: University of California Press).
Berle, Adolph A., and Means, Gardner C. 1932. *The Modern Corporation and Private Property* (New York: Macmillan).
Boot, Max. 2003. *The Savage Wars of Peace: Small Wars and the Rise of American Power* (New York: Basic Books).

Boston, Jonathan, and Martin, John, et al. 1996. *Public Management: The New Zealand Model* (Auckland, NZ: Oxford University Press).

Bosworth, Barry P., and Triplett, Jack E. 2000. *Productivity in the Services Sector* (Washington, DC: Brookings Institution).

Brown, John Seely, and Duguid, Paul. 2000. *The Social Life of Information* (Boston: Harvard Business School Press).

Buchanan, James M., and Tollison, Robert D. 1972. *The Theory of Public Choice: Political Applications of Economics* (Ann Arbor, MI: University of Michigan Press).

Buchanan, James M., Tollison, Robert D., Tullock, Gordon, et al. 1980. *Toward a Theory of a Rent-Seeking Society* (College Station, TX: Texas A&M Press).

Carpenter, Ted Galen. 1997. *Delusions of Grandeur: The United Nations and Global Intervention* (Washington, DC: CATO Institute).

Chandler, Alfred D. 1977. *The Visible Hand: The Managerial Revolution in American Business* (Cambridge, MA: Harvard University Press).

Coase, Ronald H. 1937. "The Nature of the Firm," *Economica* 6: 386–405.

Cohen, Michael D., and March, James G., et al. 1972. "A Garbage Can Model of Organizational Choice," *Administrative Science Quarterly* 17(1): 1–25.

Cohen, Theodore. 1987. *Remaking Japan: The American Occupation As New Deal* (New York: Free Press).

Cowhey, Peter F., and Haggard, Stephan. 2001. *Presidents, Parliaments, and Policy* (Cambridge, England: Cambridge University Press).

Crocker, Chester. 2003. "Engaging Failing States," *Foreign Affairs* 82 (5): 32–45.

Cyert, Richard M., and March, James G., et al. 1963. *A Behavioral Theory of the Firm* (Englewood Cliffs, NJ: Prentice-Hall).

Damrosch, Lori F. 1993. *Enforcing Restraint: Collective Intervention in Internal Conflicts* (New York: Council on Foreign Relations).

de Soto, Hernando. 2000. *The Mystery of Capital: Why Capitalism Triumphs in the West and Fails Everywhere Else* (London: Bantam Press).

——. 1989. *The Other Path: The Invisible Revolution in the Third World* (New York: Harper & Row).

Diamond, Larry, 1992. "Economic Development and Democracy Reconsidered," *American Behavioral Scientist* 15(4–5): 450–99.

——. 1990. "Three Paradoxes of Democracy," *Journal of Democracy* 1(3): 48–60.

Dobbins, James, et al. 2003. *America's Role in Nation-Building: From Germany to Iraq* (Santa Monica, CA: Rand).

Dower, John W. 1999. *Embracing Defeat: Japan in the Wake of World War II* (New York: W. W. Norton).

Doyle, Michael W., Johnstone, Ian, et al. 1997. *Keeping the Peace: Multidimensional UN Operations in Cambodia and El Salvador* (Cambridge, England: Cambridge University Press).

Easterly, William R. 2001. *The Elusive Quest for Growth: Economists' Adventures and Misadventures in the Tropics* (Cambridge, MA: MIT Press).

Einhorn, Jessica. 2001. "The World Bank's Mission Creep," *Foreign Affairs* 80(5): 22–35.

Ellickson, Robert C. 1991. *Order without Law: How Neighbors Settle Disputes* (Cambridge, MA: Harvard University Press).

Evans, Peter B. 1989. "Predatory, Developmental, and other Apparatuses: A Comparative Analysis of the Third World State," *Sociological Forum* 4(4): 561–82.

———. 1997. "The Eclipse of the State? Reflections on Stateness in an Era of Globalization," *World Politics* 50: 62–87.

Fama, Eugene F. 1980. "Agency Problems and the Theory of the Firm," *Journal of Political Economy* 88(2):288–307.

Fatton, Robert. 1992. *Predatory Rule: State and Civil Society in Africa* (Boulder, CO: Lynne Rienner Press).

Friedrich, Carl J., and Brzezinski, Zbigniew. 1965. *Totalitarian Dictatorship and Autocracy, 2d ed.* (Cambridge, MA: Harvard University Press).

Fukuyama, Francis 2004. "Nation-building 101," *The Atlantic Monthly* 293(1): 159–162.

———. 2000. *Social Capital and Civil Society* (Washington, DC: International Monetary Fund Working Paper WP/00/74).

———. 1999. *The Great Disruption: Human Nature and the Reconstitution of Social Order* (New York: Free Press).

Fukuyama, Francis, and Marwah, Sanjay. 2000. "Comparing East Asia and Latin America: Dimensions of Development," *Journal of Democracy* 11(4):80–94.

Furubotn, Eirik G., and Richter, Rudolf. 1997. *Institutions and Economic Theory: The Contribution of the New Institutional Economics* (Ann Arbor, MI: University of Michigan Press).

Greif, Avner. 1993. "Contract Enforceability and Economic Institutions in Early Trade: The Maghribi Traders' Coalition," *American Economic Review* 83(3): 525–48.

Grindle, Merilee S. 2000. *Audacious Reforms: Institutional Inven-*

tion and Democracy in Latin America (Baltimore: Johns Hopkins University Press).

——. 1996. *Challenging the State: Crisis and Innovation in Latin America and Africa* (New York: Cambridge University Press).

——. 1997. *Getting Good Government: Capacity Building in the Public Sector of Developing Countries* (Cambridge, MA: Harvard Institute For International Development).

Gwartney, James, and Lawson, Robert et al. 2002. *Economic Freedom of the World; 2002 Annual Report* (Washington, DC: Cato Institute).

Haggard, Stephan. 2000. *The Political Economy of the Asian Financial Crisis* (Washington, DC: Institute for International Economics).

Haggard, Stephan, and Kaufman, Robert R. 1995. *The Political Economy of Democratic Transitions* (Princeton University Press).

Haggard, Stephan, and McCubbins, Mathew D. 2001. *Presidents, Parliaments, and Policy* (Cambridge, England: Cambridge University Press).

Harriss, John, and Hunter, Janet, et al. 1995. *The New Institutional Economics and Third World Development* (London: Routledge).

Hartcher, Peter. 1998. *The Ministry* (Boston: Harvard Business School Press).

Hassner, Pierre 2002. "Definitions, Doctrines, Divergences," *National Interest* No. 69 (fall): 30–34.

Hayek, Friedrich A. 1956. *The Road to Serfdom* (Chicago: University of Chicago Press).

——. 1945. "The Use of Knowledge," *American Economic Review* 35(4): 519–30.

Heiberg, Marianne, 1994. *Subduing Sovereignty: Sovereignty and the Right to Intervene* (London: Pinter Publishers).

Herbst, Jeffery. 2000. *States and Power in Africa* (Princeton, NJ: Princeton University Press).

Hirschman, Albert O. 1970. *Exit, Voice, and Loyalty: Responses to Decline in Firms, Organizations, and States* (Cambridge, MA: Harvard University Press).

Hoffmann, Stanley. 1996. *The Ethics and Politics of Humanitarian Intervention* (Notre Dame, IN: University of Notre Dame Press).

Holmstrom, Bengt, and Milgrom, Paul. 1991. "Multitask Principal-Agent Analyses: Incentive Contracts, Asset Ownership, and Job Design," *Journal of Law, Economics, and Organization* 7: 24–52.

Horowitz, Donald 1990. "Comparing Democratic Systems," *Journal of Democracy* 1(4): 73–79.

Howard, Philip K. 1996. *The Death of Common Sense* (New York: Warner Books).

Huntington, Samuel P. 1968. *Political Order in Changing Societies* (New Haven: Yale University Press).

———. 1981. *American Politics: The Promise of Disharmony* (Cambridge, MA: Harvard University Press).

———. 1991. *The Third Wave: Democratization in the Late Twentieth Century* (Oklahoma City: University of Oklahoma Press).

———. 1996. *The Clash of Civilizations and the Remaking of World Order* (New York: Simon and Schuster).

Ignatieff, Michael. 2003. "The Burden," *New York Times Magazine*: (Jan 5): 162.

Ikenberry, G. John, and Hall, John A. 1989. *The State* (Minneapolis: University of Minnesota Press).

Israel, Arturo. 1987. *Institutional Development: Incentives to Performance* (Baltimore: Johns Hopkins University Press).

Jensen, Michael. 1998. *Foundations of Organizational Strategy* (Cambridge, MA: Harvard University Press).

Jensen, Michael, and Meckling, William. 1976. "Theory of the Firm: Managerial Behavior, Agency Costs, and Ownership Structure," *Journal of Financial Economics* 3: 304–60.

Johnson, Chalmers. 1982. *MITI and the Japanese Miracle* (Stanford, CA: Stanford University Press).

Joseph, Richard. 1987. *Democracy and Prebendal Politics in Nigeria: The Rise and Fall of the Second Republic* (Cambridge, England: Cambridge University Press).

Kagan, Robert. 2003. *Of Paradise and Power: America vs. Europe in the New World Order* (New York: Knopf).

Katzenstein, Peter. 1997. *Tamed Power: Germany in Europe* (Ithaca, NY: Cornell University Press).

Kaufman, Daniel, Kraay, Aart, and Mastruzzi, Massimo, *Governance Matters III: Governance Indicators for 1996–2002* (draft; Washington: World Bank, June 30, 2003). Available at www.worldbank.org/wbi/governance/pdf/govmatters3.pdf.

Klitgaard, Robert E. 1995. *Institutional Adjustment and Adjusting to Institutions* (Washington, DC: World Bank).

Knaus, Gerald, and Martin, Felix. 2003. "Travails of the European Raj," *Journal of Democracy* 14(3): 60–74.

Krasner, Stephen D. 1984. "Approaches to the State: Alternative Conceptions and Historical Dynamics," *Comparative Politics* 16(2): 223–46.

Krueger, Anne. 1993. *Political Economy of Policy Reform in Developing Countries* (Cambridge, MA: MIT Press).

———. 1974. "The Political Economy of the Rent-Seeking Society," *The American Economic Review* 64(3): 291–303.

Kupchan, Charles A. 2002. *The End of the American Era: U.S. Foreign Policy and the Geopolitics of the Twenty-first Century* (New York: Knopf).

Lanyi, Anthony, and Lee, Young. 1999. *Governance Aspects of the East Asian Financial Crisis* (College Park, MD: IRIS Working Paper 226).

Levitt, Barbara, and March, James G. "Chester I. Barnard and the Intelligence of Learning," in Oliver Williamson, ed. 1990. *Organization Theory from Chester Barnard to the Present* (New York: Oxford University Press).

Levy, Brian. 2002. *Patterns of Governance in Africa* (Washington, DC: World Bank).

Lijphart, Arend 1996. "Constitutional Choices for New Democracies," in Marc Plattner and Larry Diamond, eds., The Global Resurgence of Democracy (Baltimore: Johns Hopkins University Press).

Linz, Juan J. 1990. "The Perils of Presidentialism," *Journal of Democracy* 1(1): 51–69.

Lipset, Seymour Martin. 1995. *American Exceptionalism: A Double-Edged Sword* (New York: W. W. Norton).

——. 1990. *Continental Divide: The Values and Institutions of the United States and Canada* (New York: Routledge).

——. 1981. *Political Man: The Social Bases of Politics*, 2d ed. (Baltimore: Johns Hopkins University Press).

——. 1959. "Some Social Requisites of Democracy: Economic Development and Political Legitimacy," *American Political Science Review* 53: 69–105.

Lugo, Luis E. 1996. *Sovereignty at the Crossroads? Morality and International Politics in the Post-Cold War Era* (Lanham, MD: Rowman and Littlefield).

MacIntyre, Andrew. 2003. *The Power of Institutions: Political Architecture and Governance* (Ithaca, NY: Cornell University Press).

Malone, Thomas W., and Yates, Joanne, et al. 1987. "Electronic Markets and Electronic Hierarchies," *Communications of the ACM* 30(6): 484–97.

March, James G., and Cohen, Michael D. 1974. *Leadership and Ambiguity: The American College President* (New York: McGraw-Hill, 1974).

Marshall, S.L.A. 1947. *Men Against Fire: The Problem of Battle Command in Future War* (New York: William Morrow and Co.).

Mastanduno, Michael, and Lyons, Gene M. 1995. *Beyond Westphalia? State Sovereignty and International Intervention* (Baltimore: Johns Hopkins University Press).

Mayall, James. 1996. *The New Interventionism 1991–1994* (Cambridge, England: Cambridge University Press).

Mearsheimer, John J. 2002. "Hearts and Minds," *National Interest* (69): 13–16.

Mendelson Forman, Johanna . 2002. "Achieving Socioeconomic Well-Being in Postconflict Settings," *Washington Quarterly* 25(4): 128–38.

Miller, Gary J. 1992. *Managerial Dilemmas: The Political Economy of Hierarchy* (New York: Cambridge University Press).

Moe, Terry. 1984. "The New Economics of Organization," *American Journal of Political Science* 28: 739–77.

Murphy, Sean D. 1996. *Humanitarian Intervention: The United Nations in an Evolving World Order* (Philadelphia: University of Pennsylvania Press).

National Security Strategy of the United States of America, September 2002 (Washington, D.C.).

Nettl, J. P. 1968. "The State as a Conceptual Variable," *World Politics* 20(4): 559–92.

New Zealand State Services Commission, 1998. *New Zealand's State Sector Reform: A Decade of Change* (http://www.ssc.govt.nz/display/document.asp?docid=2384)

North, Douglass C. 1990. *Institutions, Institutional Change, and Economic Performance* (New York: Cambridge University Press).

North, Douglass C., and Weingast, Barry R. 1989. "Constitutions and Commitment: The Evolution of Institutions Governing Public Choice in Seventeenth-Century England," *Journal of Economic History* 49(4): 803–32.

Olsen, Johan P., and March, James G., et al. 1976. *Ambiguity and Choice in Organizations* (Bergen, Norway: Universitets-forlagen).

Olson, Mancur. 1996. "Big Bills Left on the Sidewalk: Why Some Nations are Rich and Others Poor," *Journal of Economic Perspectives* 10(2): 3–24.

Piore, Michael J., and Sabel, Charles. 1984. *The Second Industrial Divide* (New York: Basic Books).

Porter, Bruce D. 1994. *War and the Rise of the State: The Military Foundations of Modern Politics* (New York: Free Press).

Posner, Richard A. 1975. "The Social Costs of Monopoly and Regulation," *Journal of Political Economy* 83(4): 807–28.

Przeworski, Adam, and Alvarez, Michael, et al. 1996. "What Makes Democracies Endure?" *Journal of Democracy* 7(1): 39–55.

Quester, George H. 1973. *Nuclear Diplomacy: The First Twenty-Five Years*, 2d ed (New York: Dunellen).

Rabkin, Jeremy. 1998. *Why Sovereignty Matters* (Washington, DC: American Enterprise Institute).

Ricks, Thomas E. 1997. *Making the Corps* (New York: Scribners).

Robinson, James A., Acemoglu, Daron, et al. 2000. *The Colonial Ori-*

gins of Comparative Development: An Empirical Investigation (Washington, DC: National Bureau of Economic Research working paper 7771).

Rodrik, Dani. 1997. *Has Globalization Gone Too Far?* (Washington, DC: Institute for International Economics).

Roll, Richard, and Talbott, John R. 2003. "Political Freedom, Economic Liberty, and Prosperity," *Journal of Democracy* 14(3): 75–90.

Rose-Ackerman, Susan. 1979. *Corruption: A Study in Political Economy* (New York: Academic Press).

Rowen, Henry S. 1995. The Tide Underneath the "Third Wave," *Journal of Democracy* 6(1): 53–64.

Saiegh, Sebastian, and Tommasi, Mariano 1998. *Argentina's Federal Fiscal Institutions: A Case Study in the Transaction-Lost Theory of Politics* (Buenos Aires: Fundacion Gobiero y Sociedad).

Sakakibara, Eisuke. 1993. *Beyond Capitalism: The Japanese Model of Market Economics* (Lanham, MD: University Press of America).

Schein, Edgar H. 1988. *Organizational Culture and Leadership* (San Francisco: Jossey-Bass).

Schick, Allen. 1996. *The Spirit of Reform: Managing the New Zealand State Sector in a Time of Change* (Wellington, New Zealand: State Services Commission and the Treasury).

Scott, James C. 1998. *Seeing Like a State: How Certain Schemes to Improve the Human Conditions Have Failed* (New Haven, CT: Yale University Press).

Selznick, Philip 1951. *TVA and the Grass Roots: A Study in the Sociology of Formal Organizations* (New York: McGraw-Hill).

——. 1957. *Leadership in Administration: A Sociological Interpretation* (White Plains, NY: Peterson & Co.).

Sen, Amartya K. 1999. *Development as Freedom* (New York: Knopf).

Shefter, Martin. 1993. *Political Parties and the State: The American Historical Experience* (Princeton, NJ: Princeton University Press).

Simon, Herbert. 1957. *Administrative Behavior: A Study of Decision-Making Processes in Administrative Organization* (New York: Free Press).

Simon, Herbert, and March, James G. 1958. *Organizations* (New York: Wiley).

——. 1991. "Organizations and Markets," *Journal of Economic Perspectives* 5(2): 25–44.

Simon, Herbert, March, James G., and Smithburg, Donald W., et al. 1961. *Public Administration* (New York: Knopf).

Singerman, Diane. 1995. *Avenues of Participation: Family, Politics, and Networks in Urban Quarters of Cairo* (Princeton, NJ: Princeton University Press).

Sorensen, Georg. 2001. "War and State-Making: Why Doesn't It Work in the Third World?" *Security Dialogue* 32(3): 341–54.

Steele, Jonathan. 2002. "Nation Building in East Timor," *World Policy Journal* 19(2): 76–87.

Stiglitz, Joseph E. 2002. *Globalization and its Discontents* (New York: W. W. Norton).

Taylor, Frederick Winslow. 1911. *The Principles of Scientific Management* (New York: Harper Brothers).

Tendler, Judith. 1997. *Good Government in the Tropics* (Baltimore: Johns Hopkins University Press).

———. 1975. *Inside Foreign Aid* (Baltimore: Johns Hopkins University Press).

Tilly, Charles. 1975. *The Formation of National States in Western Europe* (Princeton, NJ: Princeton University Press).

Tullock, Gordon. 1965. *The Politics of Bureaucracy* (Washington, DC: Public Affairs Press).

United Nations Development Program. 2002. *Arab Human Development Report 2002* (New York: UNDP).

van de Walle, Nicolas. 2001. *African Economies and the Politics of Permanent Crisis, 1979–1999* (Cambridge, England: Cambridge University Press).

von Lipsey, Roderick K. 1997. *Breaking the Cycle: A Framework for Conflict Intervention* (New York: St. Martin's Press).

von Mises, Ludwig. 1981. *Socialism: An Economic and Sociological Analysis* (Indianapolis: Liberty Classics).

Weber, Max. 1946. *From Max Weber: Essays in Sociology* (New York: Oxford University Press).

Weingast, Barry R., and Moran, Mark. 1983. "Bureaucratic Discretion or Congressional Control: Regulatory Policymaking by the Federal Trade Commission," *Journal of Political Economy* 91: 765–800.

———. 1993. "Constitutions as Governance Structures: The Political Foundations of Secure Markets," *Journal of Institutional and Theoretical Economics* 149: 286–311.

———. 1984. "The Congressional-Bureaucratic System: A Principal-Agent Perspective," *Public Choice* 44: 147–92.

Weirs, Thomas, and Collins, Cindy. 1996. *Humanitarian Challenges and Interventions: World Politics and the Dilemmas of Help* (Boulder, Colo.: Westview Press).

Wildavsky, Aaron. 1990. "A Double Security: Federalism as Competition," *Cato Journal* 990: 39–58.

Williamson, John. 1994. *The Political Economy of Policy Reform* (Washington, DC: Institute for International Economics).

Williamson, Oliver E. 1975. *Markets and Hierarchies: Analysis and Antitrust Implications* (New York: Free Press).

——. 1985. *The Economic Institutions of Capitalism* (New York: Free Press).

——. 1993. *The Nature of the Firm: Origins, Evolution and Development* (Oxford, England: Oxford University Press).

Williamson, Roger. 1998. *Some Corner of a Foreign Field: Intervention and World Order* (New York: St. Martin's Press).

Wilson, James Q. 1989. *Bureaucracy: What Government Agencies Do and Why They Do It* (New York: Basic Books).

Woolcock, Michael, and Pritchett, Lant. 2002. *Solutions When the Solution is the Problem: Arraying the Disarray in Development* (Washington, DC: Center for Global Development Paper 10).

World Bank. 2002. *Building Institutions for Markets. World Development Report 2002* (New York: Oxford University Press

——. 2000. *Reforming Public Institutions and Strengthening Governance* (Washington, DC: World Bank).

World Bank. 1997. *The State in a Changing World* (Oxford, England: Oxford University Press).

Zakaria, Fareed. 2003. *The Future of Freedom: Illiberal Democracy at Home and Abroad* (New York: W. W. Norton).

INDEX

133